"For decades Os Guinness has been one of the most nuanced, realistic, yet hopeful voices calling Christians to engagement with culture. This latest volume from him should not be missed by anyone. Os summarizes some of the most helpful recent discussions, updates many of his own lifelong challenges to the church and provides many fresh insights. Highly recommended."
Tim Keller, Redeemer Presbyterian Church, New York City

"Os Guinness has written another terrific book, at once a zinging indictment of cultural idolatry in the Christian West and a clarion call to renewal on the model of Christ in the Gospels and the witness of the apostles. This is a highly readable, big-picture book, eminently suitable for discussion in groups, not least because it calls for a collective examination of conscience. His incisive eloquence and lucid prose, his witty, trenchant turn of phrase and zest for critical and theological realism mark this little volume as vintage Guinness; his call to a renaissance of authentic evangelical Christianity will renew in many their will to hope in a dark time, *spero in Deo*."
David Lyle Jeffrey, Distinguished Professor of Literature and the Humanities, Honors College, Baylor University

"This is a profound, realistic and hopeful book that reminds us that even in the darkest times the power of the gospel can change the world. Guinness issues a clarion call to the Christian West to take up the battle against secularization by refusing to be conformed to the spirit of the age. We do not isolate ourselves from culture. Rather, Guinness calls for renewal: in our confidence in God, in the power of the gospel and in the great truths of Scripture, even as we engage with the world around us. No other writer I know offers such a rich background of astute cultural analysis combined with a deep understanding of history. I finished this book feeling a deep sense of hope, which was fortified by his powerful prayers at the end of each chapter. If we heed the wisdom in this marvelous book, we could well become effective agents for Christ for such a time as this."
Rebecca Manley Pippert, speaker and author of *Hope Has Its Reasons*

"How we see the world shapes what we do in the world. Unfortunately many in the West have lost the ability to see our culture through the lenses of history and Christian faith, and God's people oscillate between cultural captivity or fearful activism. Thankfully Christ has given us church leaders like Os Guinness to restore our sight. Drawing from history, Scripture and his own experience of global Christianity, Os helps us see our present circumstances in the right light. He illuminates why the catastrophizing done by many Christians amid cultural change is unwarranted, but also soberly addresses the genuine challenges we face with new clarity and gravity. Most helpful of all, Os directs our sight back to Christ, the author and completer of our faith, in whom we find both the courage and the resources to be his people in our time. You will not regret a single minute invested in this book."

Skye Jethani, executive editor of *Leadership Journal* and author of *Futureville*

"Drawing on his years of perceptive cultural analysis and his wide understanding of history, Os Guinness issues a penetrating call to the Christian church to take up the battle against the deep inroads of secularization by refusing to be conformed to the spirit of the age. This book encourages us to learn from the past and avoid repeating its mistakes, to be aware of the oft-forgotten influence of Christianity on Western culture and to engage more deeply with the truths of Scripture. It rightly argues for a return to God, not to an era, and sees our only hope in a return to the confidence in God and his power that characterized the early Christians, whose lives were defined by their fundamental credo: 'Jesus Christ is Lord.'"

J. C. Lennox, professor of mathematics, University of Oxford, fellow in mathematics and philosophy of science, Green Templeton College

RENAISSANCE

THE POWER OF THE GOSPEL
HOWEVER DARK THE TIMES

OS GUINNESS

IVP Books

An imprint of InterVarsity Press
Downers Grove, Illinois

InterVarsity Press
P.O. Box 1400, Downers Grove, IL 60515-1426
World Wide Web: www.ivpress.com
Email: email@ivpress.com

InterVarsity Press® is the book-publishing division of InterVarsity Christian Fellowship/USA®, a movement of students and faculty active on campus at hundreds of universities, colleges and schools of nursing in the United States of America, and a member movement of the International Fellowship of Evangelical Students. For information about local and regional activities, write Public Relations Dept., InterVarsity Christian Fellowship/USA, 6400 Schroeder Rd., P.O. Box 7895, Madison, WI 53707-7895, or visit the IVCF website at www.intervarsity.org.

All Scripture quotations, unless otherwise indicated, are taken from the New American Standard Bible®, copyright 1960, 1962, 1963, 1968, 1971, 1972, 1973, 1975, 1977, 1995 by The Lockman Foundation. Used by permission.

While all stories in this book are true, some names and identifying information in this book have been changed to protect the privacy of the individuals involved.

"An Evangelical Manifesto" is copyright ©2008 by the Evangelical Manifesto Steering Committee. Used by permission.

Published in association with the literary agency of Wolgemuth & Associates.

Cover design: Cindy Kiple
Interior design: Beth Hagenberg
Images: wallpaper design: Gold and Red Sunflower Wallpaper Design by William Morris. Private
    Collection. The Stapleton Collection. The Bridgeman Art Library.
    swallow: © NNehring/iStockphoto
    border illustration: © Electric_Crayon/iStockphoto

ISBN 978-0-8308-3671-0 (print)
ISBN 978-0-8308-9657-8 (digital)

Printed in the United States of America ∞

Library of Congress Cataloging-in-Publication Data

Guinness, Os.
Renaissance : the power of the gospel however dark the times / Os
Guinness.
    pages cm
Includes bibliographical references and index.
ISBN 978-0-8308-3671-0 (pbk. : alk. paper)
1. Consolation. 2. Christianity. 3. Evangelicalism. 4.
Suffering—Religious aspects—Christianity. 5. Hope—Religious
aspects—Christianity. I. Title.
BV4905.3.G855 2014
261—dc23
                                  2014013482

DOM

and to Jenny,

whose faith and prayers

outweigh my feeble words by far.

The hand of the LORD was upon me, and He brought me out by
the Spirit of the LORD and set me down in the middle of
the valley; and it was full of bones.

He caused me to pass among them round about, and behold,
there were very many on the surface of the valley; and lo,
they were very dry.

He said to me, "Son of man, can these bones live?" And I
answered, "O Lord GOD, You know." Again He said to me,
"Prophesy over these bones and say to them, 'O dry bones,
hear the word of the LORD.'

Thus says the Lord GOD to these bones, 'Behold, I will cause
breath to enter you that you may come to life.

I will put sinews on you, make flesh grow back on you, cover
you with skin and put breath in you that you may come
alive; and you will know that I am the LORD.'"

So I prophesied as I was commanded; and as I prophesied, there
was a noise, and behold, a rattling; and the bones came
together, bone to its bone.

And I looked, and behold, sinews were on them, and flesh grew
and skin covered them; but there was no breath in them.

Then He said to me, "Prophesy to the breath, prophesy, son of
man, and say to the breath, 'Thus says the Lord GOD,
"Come from the four winds, O breath, and breathe on these
slain, that they come to life."'"

So I prophesied as He commanded me, and the breath came into
them, and they came to life and stood on their feet, an
exceedingly great army.

EZEKIEL 37:1-10

Revive thy Church, O Lord, beginning with me.

ST. AUGUSTINE, 5TH CENTURY

I cry, I cry, and I cry again. The religion of Christ, the true faith, has fallen so low that it is an object of scorn not only to the Devil but to Jews and Saracens and pagans. . . . These keep their law as they believe it, but we, intoxicated with the love of the world, have deserted our law.

St. Gregory, 11ᵀᴴ century

The sort of men who now live cannot stand anything so strong as the Christianity of the New Testament (they would die of it or lose their minds), just in the same sense that children cannot stand drink, for which reason we prepare for them a little lemonade—and official Christianity is lemonade-twaddle for the sort of beings that are now called men, it is the strongest thing they stand, and this twaddle then is their language they call "Christianity," just as children call their lemonade "wine."

Søren Kierkegaard, 19ᵀᴴ century

Verily there is that which is more contrary to Christianity, and to the very nature of Christianity, than any heresy and schism, more contrary than all heresies and all schisms combined, and that is to play Christianity.

Søren Kierkegaard, 19ᵀᴴ century

Anxious yet not disconsolate, we stand to one side for a moment, as contemplative bystanders to whom it has been granted to witness these great struggles and transitions. Oh! It is the magic of these struggles that whoever observes them must also enter into the fray!

Friedrich Nietzsche, 19ᵀᴴ century

How many times has civilisation, by which I mean a state of society where moral force begins to escape the tyranny of physical forces, climbed the ladder of Progress and been dragged down?

Winston Churchill, 20ᵗʰ century

At least five times . . . the Faith has to all appearances gone to the dogs. In each of these five cases, it was the dog that died.

G. K. Chesterton, 20ᵗʰ century

Turning and turning in the widening gyre,
The falcon cannot hear the falconer.
Things fall apart; the centre cannot hold.
Mere anarchy is loosed upon the world.
The blood-dimmed tide is loosed, and the
Ceremony of innocence is drowned.
The best lose all conviction, and the worst
Are full of passionate intensity.

W. B. Yeats, "The Second Coming," 20ᵗʰ century

The task of redeeming Western society rests in a peculiar sense upon Christianity.

Reinhold Niebuhr, 20ᵗʰ century

Sometimes I even think it is already too late. At any rate, if by the mercy of God we are to have some further breathing space, if He does grant us another chance to build up a new European civilisation on the ruins of the old, facing all the time the possibility of an imminent end to all civilised life on this globe, Christianity has a tremendous responsibility.

Emil Brunner, 20ᵗʰ century

It is hard for those who live near a Bank
To doubt the security of their money.
It is hard for those who live near a Police Station
To believe in the triumph of violence.
Do you think that the Faith has conquered the World
And that lions no longer need keepers?
Do you need to be told that whatever has been, can still be?
Do you need to be told that even such modest attainments
As you can boast in the way of polite society
Will hardly survive the Faith to which they owe their
      significance?

T. S. ELIOT, "THE ROCK," 20TH CENTURY

There still remains only God to protect man against man. Either
we will serve him in spirit and in truth or we shall enslave our-
selves ceaselessly, more and more, to the monstrous idol that we
have made with our own hands to our own image and likeness.

ETIENNE GILSON, 20TH CENTURY

In proportion as a society relaxes its hold upon the eternal, it
ensures the corruption of the temporal. All earthly civilizations
are indeed corruptible and must one day perish, the pax Bri-
tannica no less than the pax romana, and Christendom no less
than Babylon and Troy. But if most have perished prematurely, it
was largely as victims of their own proud illusions. And if our
Western civilization is to prove more durable, it can only be in
the strength of this more chastened estimate of its own majesty
and this knowledge that "here we have no continuing city."

JOHN BAILLIE, 20TH CENTURY

The Roman Empire was faced by the same vital problem as Europe today. Its relatively high standard of material civilization had become a source of vital degeneration rather than of social progress. The life was passing out of the old City-State and its institutions, and in its place there had arisen a standardized cosmopolitan mass hedonism. The State-provided pleasures of the baths, the circus, and the amphitheater gave the majority the luxuries that had formerly been the privilege of the few, and compensated them for the loss of civic freedom and honor. The citizen need no longer be a soldier, for he could pay the peasant and the barbarian to serve as mercenaries and he need no longer work, for that was the business of the slaves. And so the land decayed and the cities multiplied, producing everywhere from the Atlantic to the Euphrates the same pattern of social life—a leisure state in which the Mediterranean peoples gradually lost their vital energy and became sterile and senile.

CHRISTOPHER DAWSON, 20ᵀᴴ CENTURY

Can this miracle be repeated in a world that has for the second time grown cold? Can the Word of Life once more enlighten the darkness of a civilization that is infinitely richer and more powerful than that of pagan Rome but which seems equally to have lost its sense of direction and to be threatened with social degeneration and spiritual disintegration?

It is obvious that the Christian must answer in the affirmative. Yet on the other hand he must not look for a quick and easy solution to a problem on which the whole future of humanity depends.

CHRISTOPHER DAWSON, 20ᵀᴴ CENTURY

Contents

1

OUR AUGUSTINIAN MOMENT

C an it be that after two thousand years "This too shall pass" is finally being written over the Christian faith too? Is the Christian church finished and the Christian faith headed for the great museum of history, as the enemies of the faith now charge and certain trends in the West now seem to indicate?

"Great Pan is dead," Plutarch once wrote, describing the lament of passengers sailing along the west coast of Greece. The god of shepherds and flocks had died, and the Christian faith had triumphed over paganism. But now the church's critics are returning the compliment. From Friedrich Nietzsche's famous cry "God is dead" in the late nineteenth century to the strident claims of the "end of faith" from the new atheists in the early twenty-first century, we hear it announced again and again that the best days of the Christian faith are over. It too is nearing its end in the advanced modern world it has helped to create.

Are the current defectors from the faith prescient, then, and are we who have stayed merely diehard partisans of lost causes and sinking ships? Has modernity finally done what no enemy or persecutor has ever succeeded in doing and reduced the authority of the Scriptures to a shifting weather vane and the church to babbling impotence? And if the church is in such a sorry state in the advanced modern world, is this the hour for the final triumph of atheism, or for a victorious thrust in the resurgence of Islam? Will the now-vibrant church in the Global South fall into captivity in its turn when she too faces the challenge of modernity, so that the devil's triumph is complete?

These questions come together with a sharp question for Christians in the global era: Can the Christian church in the advanced modern world be renewed and restored even now and be sufficiently changed to have a hope of again changing the world through the power of the gospel? Or is all such talk merely whistling in the dark—pointless, naive and irresponsible?

Let there be no wavering in our answer. Such is the truth and power of the gospel that the church can be revived, reformed and restored to be a renewing power in the world again. There is no question that the good news of Jesus has effected powerful personal and cultural change in the past. There is no question too that it is still doing so in many parts of the world today. By God's grace it will do so again even here in the heart of the advanced modern world where the Christian church is presently in sorry disarray.

But of course that answer cannot just be stated baldly and left there. That would be a cheap and tinny triumphalism. The affirmative answer deserves a deeper explanation and a corresponding way of life. Any solid response must be as considered as it is confident, so that in what is genuinely a dark time for the church, our trust in God and in the gospel may be a warranted trust and not a whistling in the dark.

"At least five times," G. K. Chesterton wrote, "the Faith has to all appearances gone to the dogs. In each of these five cases, it was the dog that died."[1] The great Christian author's point is true, and a witty and bracing reminder for the downhearted. Yet we must also be sure that we understand why it is true, and why we can live and work with rock solid confidence in the gospel and confidence in the possibility of a genuine Christian renaissance however dark the times. But first let us lift up our eyes to the horizon and consider the extraordinary moment in which we live, and the full challenge it represents.

CHRISTIAN CIVILIZATION?

The great aerial combat known as the Battle of Britain proved to be one of the turning points in World War II. It began on June 18, 1940, and before and after the battle Winston Churchill, the British Prime Minister, gave two of his most famous speeches. The speech after the battle included the famous tribute to the airmen, "Never in the field of human conflict was so much owed by so many to so few." The speech before the battle is even more famous and is known today by its last five ringing words, "This was their finest hour."

But there were two sentences earlier in the speech that caused no comment at the time, but set off a lively debate after the war. What Churchill said was this: "I expect that the Battle of Britain is about to begin. Upon this battle depends the survival of Christian civilization."[2]

When the war was over, a spirited conversation took place between many of the world's most distinguished Christian thinkers, and several of them cited Churchill's words in the opening words of their essays and books. The conversation included the Anglo-American poet T. S. Eliot, the French philosopher Jacques Maritain, the English historian Christopher Dawson, the Swiss theologian Emil Brunner and the Scottish theologian John Baillie. Curiously, a similar debate had broken out after the terrible disaster of World War I, but that debate had been about civilization itself and most of the participants had no personal interest in the Christian faith. The earlier debate included such eminent intellectuals as Oswald Spengler, H. G. Wells, Arnold Toynbee and Clive Bell.

After World War II, the debate was expressly Christian and the issue was Christian civilization and the making of a distinctively Christian culture. Had the victors really shown themselves to be that "Christian"? To what extent did past eras of civilizations merit the term *Christian*? In what sense is it right for any civilization to call itself "Christian," or to be called "Christian" by others? And what were the prospects of restoring Christian culture and civilization in the future?

Seventy years later, that debate and those questions gain an added urgency from the fact that the forces of barbarism are growing uglier by the day, not only externally but internally— from the rising tide of Islamic violence, the degenerating decadence of post-Christian Western secularism, and the evident impotence and disarray of the Jewish and Christian ideas and institutions that once inspired and shaped Western civilization.

To be fair to the eminent thinkers in the original debate, they were interested in practice and not only theory, and with their historical awareness and sense of responsibility, they ranged far further afield than mere ideas. Jacques Maritain and Christopher Dawson were influential in the thinking that lay behind the Universal Declaration of Human Rights, the rise of what later became the European Union, as well as the revolutionary ideas that changed the Roman Catholic Church in Vatican II. Among the practical projects spawned at that time were the Moral Rearmament in Protestant circles, Opus Dei in Roman Catholic circles, and the Sword and Spirit in ecumenical circles. But regardless of the merits or otherwise of these initiatives, it is their debate over the core ideas of Christian civilization and culture that is so fascinating and instructive now.

With the benefit of hindsight more than half a century later, two things in their conversation stand out across the years. On the one hand, the participants clearly felt, with an intensity that has faded, to our loss, that all civilization is essentially fragile. To live in a civilized manner is an achievement that is only a thin veneer covering the rougher grain of human nature that can be exposed with a terrible suddenness. Barbarousness always lurks at some level underneath. Call the problem "original sin," as theologians have from the record of the Bible; call it the "crooked timber" of our humanity, as Immanuel Kant and Isaiah Berlin did; call it "dissonance in human form" as Nietzsche did; or call it "man's smudge" on the world, as the poet Gerard Manley Hopkins did.[3] But it means that all civilizations, whatever their momentary grandeur, have an ultimate flimsiness that is paper thin and cannot hold back the barbarism.

View Washington, DC, from the heights of Capitol Hill and ponder the lessons of all its statues, symbols and sayings. The self-proclaimed "capital of the free world" shows off nothing but an assured impression of power and permanence, and certainly nothing to suggest that American power and freedom will not last ten thousand years. Even Henry Kissinger, for all his vaunted realism and historical understanding, wrote, "At the dawn of the new millennium the United States is enjoying a preeminence unrivalled by even the greatest empires of the past."[4]

Yet view Rome from the Palatine Hill, the civilization so admired by the American founders, and the lesson is starkly different. Lying there before your eyes in the "eternal city" are the vestiges of long-gone kings, the remains of a once-proud republic, the bleached stone bones of an empire that strode the world of its time like a Colossus, and even the scattered remnants of the Egyptian and Greek civilizations that preceded Rome. Little wonder that Christopher Dawson wrote in a letter after the Second World War that all the events of the past years had convinced him "what a fragile thing civilization is, and how near we are to losing the whole inheritance."[5]

On the other hand, for all the brilliance of the post-war debaters, the depth of their discussion, their hopes and the practical initiatives they spawned, it is also clear that we today are even further from restoring Christian civilization than they were then. As will become clear, this book is emphatically not an argument for "Christian civilization," let alone Western civilization. My supreme concern is the first term rather than the second, and therefore the church rather than the civilization. But it is a point of fact that in many, if not most parts of the Western world, what was still left of the Christian foundations of the West have collapsed or are collapsing. The Christian church is on the defensive almost everywhere. The Christian faith is derided among the thought leaders of our societies, and now we are told it is being abandoned in droves—even if many of the defectors are not really atheists or even agnostic, but in limbo between the characteristic halfway houses of "believing without belonging" or still "belonging without believing."

Make no mistake. The troubles facing the Christian church in the West do not mean for a minute that the post-Christian forces in the West have triumphed for long. On the contrary, the West as a whole is in crisis, for the present moment has falsified the utopian Enlightenment hope that secular progressives placed in history. Could humanly directed history replace heaven as the vehicle of human progress and provide the guarantee of human desires for freedom, justice, peace and global order? The returns are now in after a century or two, and the contradictory facts are clear.

The West has beaten back the totalitarian pretensions of both Hitler's would-be master race in Germany and Stalin's would-be master class in the Soviet Union. But it now stands weak and unsure of itself before its three current menaces: first, the equally totalitarian, would-be master faith of Islamism from the Middle East; second, the increasingly totalitarian philosophy and zero-sum strategies of illiberal liberalism; and third, the self-destructive cultural chaos of the West's own chosen ideas and lifestyles that are destroying its identity and sapping its former strength.

Neither secular progress nor secular progressives have brought the West where they once promised. Nor can they. They are merely parasites on the Jewish and Christian beliefs and ideals that made the West the West. Progressive leaders in the West can no longer describe a future that is considered progress—except in the gee-whiz terms of technology. Nor are they any longer the unrivaled leaders of the world to take the future anywhere, and those rising to rival them show scant regard for Western progressives and their ideals. And in the process of their abortive bid to replace the Jewish and Christian ideals of the West, the post-Christian liberals have often shown themselves to be highly illiberal. Drinking deep of postcolonial guilt and espousing the philosophy of "my enemy's enemy is my friend," they have cozied up to Islam in attempt to rout the vestiges of Judaism and the Christian faith that still stand in their way. And in the process they are fast abandoning as "illusions" Jewish and Christian ideals such as human dignity, freedom and personal responsibility that were once considered essential to liberalism and progress.

None of these five brief paragraphs tells the whole story of the Western crisis, and the story is far from over. But it highlights how that post-war conversation now appears to have all the marks of a "sunset debate." Just as the sun is most glorious and most colorful as it sets, so many debates have a dramatic intensity precisely because the topic in question is disappearing from view and beyond recall. And so it might seem after a cursory reading of this remarkable post-war discussion about Christian culture and civilization.

Western cultural elites have disregarded God for more than two centuries, but for a while the effects were mostly confined to their own circles. At first, they disregarded God. Then they deliberately desecrated Western tradition and lived in ways that would have spelled disaster if they had been followed more closely. But now in the early twenty-first century, their movement from disregard to desecration to decadence is going mainstream, and the United States is only the lead society among those close to the tipping point.

Soon, as the legalization and then normalization of polyamory, polygamy, pedophilia and incest follow the same logic as that of abortion and homosexuality, the socially destructive consequences of these trends will reverberate throughout society until the social chaos is beyond recovery. We can only pray there will be a return to God and sanity before the terrible sentence is pronounced: "God has given them over" to the consequences of their own settled choices.

TO CHANGE THE WORLD

Both those earlier post-war debates came back to mind recently when a similar discussion broke out in the English-speaking world, set off by such books as James Davison Hunter's *To Change the World* and Andy Crouch's *Culture Making*. Can Christians really change the world? Are they doing so today?

On one side were the optimists, some serious, some almost blithe. For a generation now, countless Christian leaders and writers had liberally sprinkled their speeches, sermons and books with phrases such as "making a difference," "leaving a legacy," "transforming culture" and "changing the world." (One Christian university in the United States proudly trumpets the slogan, "Where world change begins," and a recent term of address in some Christian audiences has been "My fellow world-changers!") But for every thousand who have used the phrases as self-evident, there have been few who asked whether such change was actually happening, and why and how they believed that it could.

On the other side were the sober, if not the sour, realists. They rubbed in the fact that, for all the talk, the highly touted "world change" was simply not happening. Some even argued that it could not happen, considering the way the speakers were pursuing the notion. Unless Christians learned to have a better grasp of how ideas influence culture, all the well-intentioned talk of Christian ideas, a Christian mind and "thinking Christianly" would produce nothing but hot air and disillusionment.

My own position is strongly on the side of the former, though with a stiff dose of the realistic understanding of the latter. As St. Paul tartly reminded the Christians in the great cosmopolitan city of Corinth, the good news of Jesus does not come in words only, but in power. It has a proven record of being the greatest people-changing and world-changing force in history. "The thought of Christianity was to want to change everything," wrote Søren Kierkegaard. "Twelve men united on being Christians have recreated the face of the world."[6] Indeed, that transforming power is at the heart of the genius of the West, and a direct gift of the gospel with its emphasis on life change. In Christopher Dawson's words, "Western civilization has been the great ferment of change in the world, because the changing of the world became an integral part of its cultural ideal."[7]

But that transforming power is precisely what must be understood all over again, re-experienced and demonstrated once more in our time. The dynamism of the gospel and its relationship to culture must be understood and lived out on its own terms, whatever the challenges today. If the critics and the cynics are to be proved wrong, God's work must always be done in God's way to see results that are worthy of God's reality and greatness. The present moment is urgent, and there is little time to lose.

WHEN THE WORLD AS WE HAVE KNOWN IT HAS GONE

Like ants on the vast floor of the Grand Canyon, none of us can see far enough and high enough to truly know where we are in the surging course of history. Only God knows. My own best assessment is that we are in a time of momentous transition, for we are living in the twilight of five hundred years of Western dominance of the world. From the rise of the intrepid Portuguese explorers who first circumnavigated the world, through the Spanish, French, Dutch and British empires, right down to the "American century" and unacknowledged American empire, the West has recently been the strongest civilization in the world of its time, and for better or worse has imposed its will on much of the rest of the world.

To be sure, the West is still powerful and the United States is still the world's lead society, and it is Western ideas and forces, such as capitalism, science and technology, which are now shaping the globalization of the entire world. But five hundred years is a mere blink of an eye, and those powerful forces are now running on their own, with no Western moral thinking to guide them. For at this juncture, the West has cut itself off from its own Jewish and Christian roots—the faith, the ideas, the ethics and the way of life that made it the West. It now stands deeply divided, uncertain of its post-Christian identity, and with its dominance waning in the global era.

With the newly awakened ancient powers of China and India on the rise, the Middle East in convulsions, and the long-slumbering continent of Africa stirring with new promise, the days of unquestioned Western dominance are numbered. In a universe billions of years old, and compared with civilizations that lasted for thousands of years, five hundred years of dominance is a small achievement anyway. But even on our smaller human scale, we can recognize the old age that is dying, but not the new one that is being born.

We are at a truly Augustinian moment, for St. Augustine died in north Africa with the Vandals at the gates, and he had lived through the sack of Rome by the Visigoths in A.D. 410, the date that is the most celebrated milestone in the decline and fall of Rome's Western empire after eight hundred years of Roman dominance. As St. Jerome wrote famously, if melodramatically, "The light of the world was put out and the head of the Empire was cut off."[8] Surely, it was widely felt, the end of all things was at hand.

Augustine's privilege and his challenge was to trust God and live faithfully at such a time of turmoil, breakdown and distress, and to articulate a vision of the kingdom of God that could form a pathway to cross the dark ages between the collapse of Rome in the West and the centuries-later rise of Christendom.

Thus in many ways St. Augustine throws more light on our age than Karl Marx, Sigmund Freud and all our noisy new atheists combined. In Dawson's estimate, "Augustine was no mere spectator of the crisis. He was, to a far greater degree than any emperor or general or barbarian warlord, a maker of history and builder of the bridge which was to lead from the old world to the new."[9]

Or again we might say that we are at a Daniel-like moment, for Daniel and his three friends faced a challenge unlike that of most of the Jews before them. The world as the Jews had known it for hundreds of years from Joshua onward had gone. Not since the captivity in Egypt had Jews been strangers in a strange land as they found themselves when defeated and deported as exiles to Babylon in the sixth century B.C.

Yet for Daniel and his friends, there was to be no nostalgic sighing, and they did not join their fellow Jews who were famously reluctant to sing the Lord's song in a foreign land. Their task was to be faithful to God at the highest levels of the greatest empire of their day, when exile and the destruction of their homeland had torn them savagely from the world that they had known. That old world had gone, so Daniel was in Babylon and not Jerusalem, his rulers were pagan and not Jewish, his frame of thinking was the course of history and not just God's covenant with Israel, and his source of God's disclosure were dreams, visions and symbols and not just the plain authority of "Thus says the Lord."

What does our moment of transition to a post-Christian West mean for us? In the fullest sense, only God knows. In terms of the past, we can see that the world that our parents and grandparents knew has gone forever—in terms of both the dominance of the West and the unrivaled status of the Christian faith in the West. For some parts of that changed situation, we can only say good riddance because of the manifest sins of the West; and for the better parts that are no more, it is idle merely to lament. It is certainly sad to face the reasons why we have become post-Christian in the West, but at the same time it is encouraging to see that we are also in a post-Western Christian church, a worldwide church that is now global and growing, and can no longer be identified simply with the West. After half a millennium of dominance, the West is being eclipsed in the global era, the United States as the lead society in the West stands on the verge of relative if not absolute decline, and much of the Christian Church in both Europe and North America is in a sorry state of weakness, confusion, unfaithfulness and cultural captivity.

It is true that much of the drift and defections from the Western churches is a welcome and much-needed paring away of wood that has long gone rotten. When, for example, Unitarian voices are trumpeting the fact that many of the so-called religious "nones" should now identify with them, that says little except that we live in an age of doubt, disillusion and disaffiliation, which naturally prizes what has been described as "the faith that you go to when you don't know where to go to."

But what of the future? If it is true that an old age is dying and the new age is as yet unborn, are any of its features clear? Lenin used to say that a situation like this carries a "revolutionary condition." The older generation and its ways have lost their authority and are no longer able to rule, and many in the younger generation are no longer willing to be ruled as before. But that still says nothing about the contours of the future. Lenin's analysis was deliberately self-serving, and he and his fellow communists have proved as wrong in their prophecies as they were disastrous in their policies. But their follies illustrate the deeper danger of a moment like ours. As Daniel was warned centuries ago, such times breed self-appointed hotheads who attempt to fulfill self-generated visions, but only succeed in falling on their faces and dishonoring the cause of God and truth. Let us not make that mistake again. Faithfulness and orthodoxy need never be frantic. Christian extremism is little better than secularist or Muslim extremism.

IT IS HEAVEN THAT RULES

The only firm statement I would offer is that three factors will be among those that shape the world to come. The first is obvious, almost banal. The world to come will be shaped by the fact that it is truly global, as the many global trends and challenges converge and interact as never before. No serious Christian can ignore the realities and challenges of globalization.

The second factor is less obvious. The world to come will be shaped by whether the worldwide Christian church recovers its integrity and effectiveness and demonstrates a faith that can escape cultural captivity and prevail under the conditions of advanced modernity—or does not. After all, religion will always be decisive in culture, just as culture is in politics, and as the most numerous and diverse faith on earth, the Christian faith is bound to be influential in the future one way or the other— either through its faithfulness or its failure.

Let me clear about what I mean by "advanced modernity," as this term is not self-evident today when many people speak of "postmodernity" and some of "late modernity." Those who think only within a framework of philosophy and ideas would say that we are in a "postmodern" world, in the sense that the ideas of postmodernism have largely supplanted those of modernism.

That is clearly an accurate way of speaking if we confine ourselves to that narrow framework of ideas. But the term is less helpful if we enlarge our framework of thinking, as we must, and go beyond ideas to encompass the entire spirit, systems and structures of modernity, viewed as the child of the forces of the industrial revolution and globalization. From that perspective, it makes no sense to speak of "postmodernity," for short of some unimaginable catastrophe, we cannot conceive of a world beyond modernity understood in that broader way.

Similarly, I prefer the term "advanced modernity" to "late modernity" because the latter suggests a precision we do not have. Even with the very highest of our hawk's eye, human views, we simply do not know where we are in the unseen timetable of modernity.

The third factor is the unknown but all-decisive one. God is sovereign over the course of history and the rise and fall of powers. As the book of Daniel reminds us again and again, "*It is* Heaven *that* rules."[10] God is the ultimate source of all power. All human power is therefore derived, limited, unstable and transient. There is always an "after you" that marks the terminus of every great power and the transition to the next. That is true not only of Nebuchadnezzar and Babylon, Persia, Greece and Rome, but of every modern empire, superpower and great power too—the United States included. God gives power and God takes away power, especially from the arrogant. We have nothing that we did not receive, and even over the highest, strongest and most enduring that we humans ever achieve, the ancient wisdom still holds true: "This too shall pass."

The future, then, will not finally be a matter of superpower agendas, scientific discoveries, technological advances, environmental disasters, Black Swan crises that are unforeseen and unforeseeable, or even the ongoing march of human folly. The final factor in the future is unknown but sure: It lies in God's good, strong hands.

NEW CHRISTIAN RENAISSANCE

There is no shortage of analyses of the twin crises of the church and the West, but by themselves such analyses have too often led to despondency, fear and paralysis, just as medical diagnoses without remedies can be heartless and debilitating. What we also need is a constructive overarching vision of Christian engagement in today's advanced modern world, one that is shaped by faith in God and a Christian perspective rather than by current wisdom, and one that can inspire Christians to move out with courage to confront the best and worst that we may encounter.

Only God knows the outcome of the present state of affairs. He alone knows whether we are moving toward some bright new dawn of global affairs, or in W. B. Yeats's terms, "slouching toward Bethlehem," in a new dark age made "more sinister, and perhaps more protracted," as Churchill warned in the same speech, "by the lights of perverted science"—or whether we will simply muddle along somewhere in between.[11] We do not know the outcome, so we have to act in faith through the chronic obscurity of the present. What we do know, beyond a shadow of a doubt, is that we are called to "have no fear," and therefore not to indulge in what is currently the world's dominant emotion, fear. Nor are we to respond to the specter of crisis and decline with either nostalgia or despair.

What then should be our response? And what for us is the best way forward in the urgency of the present situation? There are many traditions among the followers of Jesus—the Orthodox, Catholic, Evangelical, Lutheran, Reformed, Anglican, Anabaptist and Pentecostal being only the main ones in the West. But an important fact has grown clear over the last generation. Those who are faithful and orthodox in each tradition are closer to the faithful and orthodox in other traditions than to the liberal revisionists in their own tradition. In other words, the closer we all are to Jesus, the less significant the labels that once divided us.

We therefore face a common challenge as followers of Jesus in the advanced modern world. *It is, I believe, that we trust in God and his gospel and move out confidently into the world, living and working for a new Christian renaissance, and thus challenge the darkness with the hope of Christian faith, believing in an outcome that lies beyond the horizon of all we can see and accomplish today.*

Why "renaissance" when the famous fifteenth-century Renaissance is often considered classical rather than Christian at best, and at worst openly opposed to the gospel and the church? The full picture is rather richer than any stick-like description, for the Renaissance was far more than a dry return to classical learning. It was also a rich rediscovery of human individuality, creativity, beauty, wisdom, nature and the virtues of statecraft.

So the full content of what I mean by a new Christian renaissance will emerge as we proceed. But remember some simple points at the outset.

First, there were several renaissances before the Renaissance, and the earlier ones, such as the reform movements of Peter Damian and Francis of Assisi, were expressly Christian and profoundly spiritual. Indeed, historians have described the rise of Christendom itself as "the age of Western Renaissance for it is essentially the birth of a new world culture."[12]

Second, the great sixteenth-century Reformers such as Martin Luther and John Calvin owed much to the Renaissance, and to an important degree the Reformers were Renaissance people themselves (for example, the way they used language and history rather than medieval allegories in their interpretation of Scripture).

Third, the term *renaissance* is simply the French word for rebirth, and its deepest roots—and fulfillment—go all the way back to Jesus himself and to his nighttime conversation with Nicodemus. Rebirth is essentially a Christian notion.

But the term itself is not what matters. Choose your own word. Call it renewal, call it reformation, call it restoration, call it revival, call it the simple but profound Jewish term *return*, or call it renaissance. What matters is that it is a movement that is led by the Spirit of God, which involves the people of God returning to the ways of God and so demonstrating in our time the kingdom of God, and not in word only but in power and with the plausibility of community expression. William Wilberforce captured the heart of such a Christian renaissance when—long before Mao Zedong—he said, "Let a thousand flowers bloom!"

What follows is a discussion of major themes that, taken together, make such a vision of a new Christian renaissance both realistic and urgent in our time.

A Prayer

High King of heaven, Lord of the years and sovereign over time and history, grant to us such an overpowering knowledge of who you are that our trust in you may be unshakable. Grant to us too a sufficient understanding of the signs of the times in which we live that we may know how to serve your purposes in our generation and more truly be your people in our world today. To that end, O Lord, revive us again and draw us closer to yourself and to each other. Where there is false contentment with our present condition, sow in us a holy restlessness. Where there is discouragement, grant us fresh hearts. Where there is despair, be our hope again. For your sake empower us to be your salt and light in the world, and thus your force for the true human flourishing of your shalom. In the name of Jesus, Amen.

Questions for Discussion

1. What is your assessment of the state of the church, or of the many churches, in the West today? Are you and your friends encouraged or discouraged overall? Why?

2. When you hear people talking of "making a difference" and "changing the world," and so on, is it just a clichéd shorthand, or do they know, and can they also say how it can be done?

3. What sort of baggage weighs down terms such as *revival* and *reformation* in the circles you move in? Draw up a list of the pros and cons of such terms as *renewal, awakening, revival, reformation* and *renaissance*. Which do you prefer, and why, and who are the leaders you respect who have that vision?

2

GRAND GLOBAL TASKS

The global era represents the most significant opportunity for the Christian church since the apostles and the most significant challenge for the church since the apostles.

The opportunity lies in the simple fact that the Christian faith is the world's first global religion. The challenge lies in the equally simple fact that modernity—the spirit, system and structures of the world that have risen since the Industrial Revolution—has done more damage to the Christian faith than all the persecutors in Christian history, from Nero and Diocletian to Hitler, Stalin, Mao and the assorted tyrants of today. The seductions and distortions of modernity are in fact the central reason for the sorry disarray of the church in the Western world.

The Christian church therefore stands on the verge of a historic moment in the global era, and we need to view the position of the church in the West as a crucial part, though only a small part of a far wider picture of the church in the modern world.

We call our age the global era, and the term is justified, for what the world is experiencing is far from *globaloney,* the word with which some critics dismiss globalization with a sneer. It is true that any description of globalization must always include its countervailing trends, for the world is "globalizing," "localizing" and even "glocalizing" at the same time. The European Union, for example, represents the emergence of the world's first truly supranational continent in the modern era, but at the same time many Scots want to break away from the rest of Britain and many Basques from Spain.

It is true too that globalization itself is not new, and we have to be clear as to what exactly we are claiming is new today. There have been many earlier globalizing waves throughout history. Significant examples of smaller and more limited waves are such powerful movements as religious missions (think of Buddha and Islam as well as the spread of the gospel), military conquests (think of Genghis Khan as well as Alexander the Great, Julius Caesar and Napoleon), voyages of exploration, and always the constant expansion of trading and business empires.

All of these movements "globalized" the world in their own way and in their own time, but the momentum is rapidly accelerating in our own day. Starting two hundred years ago, the Industrial Revolution represented a fresh and gigantic wave of globalization, in that it linked and transformed large parts of the earth never in close contact before. And now, even that enormous wave has been superseded in its turn by the latest and even greater wave through the globalizing power of high-tech communications.

With this latest wave in mind, we can say that the truly global era has dawned. Evidence of what we call "globalization" can be found almost everywhere, and a simple but accurate definition is that *globalization is the process by which human interconnectedness is reaching a genuinely global level*. Market capitalism is an obvious leader of the forces exploiting the new global potential, but the real driver is information technology. In particular, the current wave of globalization is thrusting forward through the so-called "3 S forces"—the speed, scale and simultaneity of information technology.

Needless to say, globalization hits our daily lives in ways that are far more concrete. This impact can be captured in the plethora of slogans commonly bandied around today: "Everyone is now everywhere." "We are the first generation to see everything as it happens." "Everything is interconnected and no one is in charge." "You can reach anywhere in the world from anywhere else, and in twenty-four hours," and so on and so on.

It is at this extraordinary moment, when the entire world is aware of the entire world as never before and because of this is facing unprecedented challenges that will be crucial for the future of humankind, that the Christian faith has risen to be the world's first truly global religion.

To claim that the Christian faith is the world's first truly global religion is not a matter of cheap triumphalism but of hard facts. There are other truly global religions, such as Buddhism and Islam. But Jesus of Nazareth has the greatest number of followers of any religion on planet Earth, the church is the most diverse community on the earth, the Bible is the most translated and translatable book in human history, churches are the most numerous social service agencies across the world, and in many parts of the world the Christian faith is the fastest growing (and most persecuted) faith—and growing through conversion rather than simply through the birth rate. And again, all this at a time of momentous significance for the future of humanity.

None of these facts are accidental. For one thing, the Christian faith, and the Jewish faith from which it springs, both have a global vision in their DNA. These two faiths were global and globalizing long before the term *globalization*. The founding call of Abraham introduces a note of universality that rings out again and again in Jewish and Christian history: "In you all the families of the earth will be blessed."[1] For Christians, Jesus' Great Commission to his followers strengthens the universality into an inescapable imperative. Christians are commanded to go through all the world and make disciples of all the nations.[2]

For another thing, it is a matter of historical record that the Christian faith has been the leading faith of the Western world, which in turn has been the main carrier of globalization in its modern forms. And as we shall see, many of the defining features of Western civilization are the direct or indirect "gifts" of the Christian faith. The gospel and modernity have therefore fanned out across the world in tandem, sometimes for better and sometimes for worse. To be sure, the chief globalizing forces of our time—capitalism, science and technology—are now largely self-justifying and self-sustaining. But even in today's world, many people first encounter modernity through influential Christian nonprofit agencies such as World Vision, Compassion International and Opportunity International rather than just through corporate products from Coca-Cola and McDonald's to Apple, Nike and Starbucks.

In short, the prospect facing the Christian church at the global level is quite different from the purely Western prospect, and far more immediately encouraging. It is in this sense that we can truly say that the global era represents the greatest opportunity for the church since the apostles and the greatest challenge for the church since the apostles. The opportunity grows from the openness for the spread of the gospel, made possible by the new media and technologies—our counterpart to the Greek language and Roman roads that facilitated the spread of the Christian message in the first century A.D. The challenge lies in the fact that most of the church's growth can be found in the largely premodern world, whereas most of the church's problems lie in its cultural captivity in the advanced modern world—supremely in the West.

For anyone who weighs the momentous significance of this situation, it highlights three major tasks the global church must undertake over the course of the twenty-first century: to prepare the Global South, to win back the Western world, and to contribute to the human future. These tasks go far wider than the immediate issue of a Christian renaissance in the Western world, but it is an inescapable feature of the global era that no task anywhere in the world can afford to ignore the wider challenges elsewhere in the world. These three global tasks must therefore form the horizon of our thinking about the more local issues and challenges we face in the West.

PREPARING THE GLOBAL SOUTH

The first grand task for the worldwide church is to help to prepare the Global South for the challenges that are coming along with the forces of development and modernization.

The story of the astonishing growth of the Christian church in the Global South is one of the great stories of our time, and it is both well documented and widely known—for example, in Philip Jenkins's *The Next Christendom* and Mark Noll's *The New Shape of World Christianity*. Most of the focus in these accounts has been on Christian expansion in sub-Saharan Africa and in Asia, especially China. For example, the growth of the churches radiating out from Henan Province in north central China is said to be the fastest growth of the Christian church in two thousand years, and it is now widely reported that there are more Christians in China than there are members of the Communist Party itself. David Martin's and Peter Berger's attention to the growth of Pentecostals and Evangelicals in South America, especially Brazil, has received less attention, but it is equally remarkable.

These reports are accurate and highly encouraging, especially when contrasted with the sorry state of the church in the West. But some of the accounts omit a single factor that is a sting in the tail for any who are celebrating mindlessly. *The churches in the Global South are largely premodern, when the poor condition of the churches in the West is largely because of their capitulation to the distorting power of modernity.* In other words, the main challenge to the churches in the Global South is yet to come, but come it surely will, and the question arises as to whether they are prepared to face the challenge.

At the moment the frank answer would have to be no. By the admission of their own leaders, much of the growth of the Christian faith in the Global South is (in the words of an African archbishop) "a mile wide and an inch deep." Evangelism is exploding, but it has not been followed up with adequate teaching and discipleship. The result, as another African bishop said to me, is that "when my people hit a problem, they revert to their pre-Christian practices. A husband finds his wife cannot bear children, so he resorts to the witch doctor, or takes a second or third wife."

A house church pastor in China made a similar comment: "Many of my people are only one unanswered prayer away from leaving the church and resorting to Buddhism or animism to solve their problems." The heroic courage of Christians standing firm under fire from the savage persecution of tyrants such as Mao Zedong has shamed the comfort-loving complacence of Western Christians. But it is an even harder thing to negotiate the challenges of modernity, and the signs are that many Christians are falling way when they move from China's rural areas to the big, teeming, bustling cities such as Beijing and Shanghai.

This means that we who are Christians in the advanced modern world have a duty to share the story of our own dealings with modernity with our sisters and brothers in the Global South who are yet to face its full impact. The overall challenge of modernity is summarized in the gravedigger thesis—the idea that the Western church was the single strongest source of the ideas that shaped the rise of the modern world, yet the Western church has become culturally captive to the world to which it gave rise. In so doing, it has become its own gravedigger.[3]

To recommend that Western Christians reach out with such advice is easier said than done, because most Christians in the West have yet to recognize, let alone analyze, their own captivity to the forces of modernity. So when we Western Christians speak to our fellow believers in the Global South, it has to be with a genuine humility and a candid confession. In essence, we have to say to our fellow Christians elsewhere, "Don't make the mistakes that we have done, and here is where we have gone badly wrong and betrayed our Lord."

This is not the place to stop and describe in detail how the modern world has squeezed the Western church into its mold so that, through its growing worldliness, the Western church has lost its decisive integrity and effectiveness. Along with others, I have attempted such an analysis in many different ways over forty years, most recently in *The Last Christian on Earth*, but let me state this briefly here. At the heart of the crisis of the church in the advanced modern world, we need to recognize how modernity has had the effect of shifting the church from an integrated faith to a fragmented faith, from a stance under authority to a stance of preferences, and from a supernatural sense of reality to a purely secular perspective.

The effect is what matters. To use the famous words of St. Paul, much of the Western church today is "conformed" rather than "transformed."[4] Or as Walter Lowrie wrote in his introduction to Kierkegaard's *Attack upon Christendom*, "The world does not persecute the world when it discovers it in the Church."[5] Theologian David Wells stands out among those incisive Christian writers who have made this critique central to their descriptions of the church and theology today.[6] Needless to say, the lessons of this modern captivity can never be translated woodenly from one culture to another. As the Global South modernizes in its own time, it will also do so in its own way—beginning with cell phones rather than steam engines, for example—and unquestionably it will be in ways that are unique and somewhat different from our Western experience.

Some of the worst forms of Western worldliness are obvious, such as our rampant individualism and consumerism, and some are already doing pernicious damage in the Global South. The vilest is the distortion of the gospel through American-style health-and-wealth theology, with its prosperity doctrines and their vicious exploitation of the unsuspecting poor. The logic and dynamics of this shameless twisting of the gospel run parallel to those of witchcraft and are equally distressing and outrageous. But Christians around the world also need to be on the lookout for many subtler forms of worldliness that are less noticed and rarely analyzed. For example, one whole range of problems stems from the features of the modern world that touch our minds and distort our Christian thinking in ways that run counter to the gospel, yet are less obvious.

To be sure, most Western Christians develop a healthy resistance to obvious intellectual menaces, such as the new atheism or relativism. These challenges are overt, explicit and hard to miss (though many are less wary of the subtler forms of syncretism that should raise equal concern). But we generally pay less attention to subtler trends that are also dangerous—such as the fashionable modern obsession with public opinion, numbers, quantity and metrics. These deserve far more thought than most

Christians give them, for they go to the heart of issues that are central to faith.

Again and again, prophets such as Elijah and Isaiah posed three essential questions to Israel: Who do you worship? (God or the gods?) In whom or what do you trust? (In God or in the superpowers and military might?) And how are you to serve God in your times? (Through power or through trust in God despite weakness?) Wrong answers to these questions, such as a reliance on a census, spelled disaster for Israel.

We are in danger of making the same mistake. To be sure, numbers are important for understanding and ordering our universe, yet only within limits. Yet what we are experiencing today is a tyranny of numbers that requires a challenge because of our misplaced trust in numbers and their illusory promise of mastery and control.

Management through metrics has become the golden road to progress in the modern world. Michael Bloomberg, when mayor of New York, governed as the ultimate metrics man who saw everything in terms of targets, yardsticks, scorecards and predictive models. "In God we trust," he used to quip. "All others bring metrics."

Again, to be sure, there is no question that numbers are accurate to a point. But whenever they appear to work, they create the illusion of greater accuracy than they have—so much so that there is no need to trust in God, or to take God into account at all. We can manage by ourselves, thank you. We can do what Jesus and the Torah said we could not do—we can live by bread alone, or least by science alone, technology alone and management by metrics alone.

America as the lead society in the modern world is awash with numbers and metrics, and with statistics, opinion polls, surveys, targets, pie charts, scorecards, big data, game theory and measurable outcomes—all at the expense of the true, the good, the beautiful, the faithful and the significant—and at the expense of God too. Numbers and the mania for metrics are therefore a critical element of secularization. Crucially for Jews and Christians, the Bible shows the link between statistics and self-trust, and our founding commands include the Sinai admonition: "You shall not follow the masses [the crowd, the many] in doing evil."[7] Called to be a separate and distinct people, our call is to the "narrow" rather than the "broad way." For followers of Jesus, the voice of the people must never be taken as the voice of God.

Nineteenth-century thinkers foresaw the rising domination of numbers, quantity and majority opinion, and warned against it. They regarded it as the overspill of the age of democratic majorities and the triumph of technocratic rationalism, through which everything would be reduced to numbers, and big numbers would be valued most of all. The pressure would therefore be toward a false notion of explanation through numbers, a dangerous authority for numbers at the expense of the true and the good, and in the end toward a disastrous strengthening of the Leviathan of the state (for what else is "big" enough and "wise" enough to coordinate and manage everyone and everything but the government?).

"In America," Alexis de Tocqueville wrote in the 1830s, "the majority builds an impregnable wall around the process of thinking."[8] Novelist James Fennimore Cooper, an American himself, wrote, "It is a besetting vice of democracies to substitute public opinion for law."[9] The philosopher John Stuart Mill warned that "the price paid for this sort of intellectual pacification is the sacrifice of the entire moral courage of the human mind."[10] Kierkegaard wrote in his journal, "The trend today is in the direction of mathematical equality."[11] In 1866, the historian Jacob Burckhardt remarked with sarcasm, "Even more serious is the steady increase of complete despair about every kind of smallness; anybody who does not belong to a nation of at least thirty million shouts: 'Help us, oh Lord, we are drowning!'"[12]

For the Hebrew prophets, "Thus says the Lord" was decisive, not the opinions of the people. And in fact, the pursuit of truth, beauty, excellence, whether in art, science or spiritual growth, has rarely taken its cue from John Q. Public or from Mr. and Mrs. Average. It aspires to the standards of the few and the exceptional—the great masters, the inspiring heroes and the extraordinary saints. Generous patrons have often been a fruitful part of the story, but grand masters, great models and generous patrons were seldom found in the crowds in their day. Lovers of truth, beauty, excellence and spiritual growth do not bother to curry favor with great numbers or any majority, and their accomplishments defy all quantifying. Too often, as Søren Kierkegaard declared, the crowd is "untruth" and "the public is chimera."[13] Or as the Stoic philosopher Seneca wrote even more bluntly, seconded later by the great Polish scientist Copernicus, "I never wanted to please the people. What the people want, I ignore, and what I know, the people do not realize."[14]

If the danger of the tyranny of numbers was evident in the nineteenth century, how much more so is it today. We are in the age of gargantuan numbers, truly instant information, ceaselessly hyperactive social media, when the World Wide Web has become a flood-driven Niagara of raw, uninterpreted information and emotion that pounds down on us by the minute with its ceaseless roar and its drenching deluge. Who can hear themselves think, let alone make sense of it all with genuine reflection and seasoned judgments?

No wonder it is tempting to give up and go with the flow, rushing along with the crowds and sweeping past the best as we chase after the most. It is all too easy to get caught up in the sensational and forget the significant. Those who make this mistake miss the important for the urgent and become attuned to popular approval rather than divine authority. They count opinions rather than weigh them. The imprimatur they covet is to be called "in," "cool," "relevant," or better still, one of "the hundred most influential" or part of a new "emerging majority." For heaven's sake, read anything and everything that is "in" at the present moment. But we must pray always and unceasingly that we are never, God forbid, "out of fashion" or fear being caught on "the wrong side of history."

And now, to make the idolatry of numbers worse, our earnest and scientifically rigorous Christian foundations lean on us heavily and require that we provide "measurable outcomes" for every project, plan and possibility that dares to knock on their door, when often the desired outcomes are quite unquantifiable, at least in advance, and at other times we can only fill in the application forms with wild guesses, wishful thinking or downright fabrications. In short, with their unfailing encouragement and blessing, we are invited either to deceive them or deceive ourselves and so become schooled in the art of lying and gaming their system to get their money. And what does the leadership of the Holy Spirit have to do with any of that?

Every age is fooled by its own fashions, and it is time to subject this modern idolatry of opinion and numbers to decisive Christian thinking. Just as humans made in the image of God are more than the chemistry of the cells that make us, so we are more than *aides de camp* to the almighty computer. We would of course scorn anyone who put their half-baked preferences, momentary whims and brazen desires above serious concerns for truth. So why do we bow to opinion polls that are mostly just such emotions gathered with statistical scientific precision and expressed under the halo of grand numbers?

Consider the trend toward numbers in light of our relationship to God. Metrics are quantitative and not qualitative, so they measure performance, but not relationships. They tell us about the externals of religion and say nothing about the heart. Metrics, for instance, can tell us what husbands spend this year on Valentine's cards and gifts for their wives, but not whether the cards and gifts express their love or their guilt at not loving their wives as they once did.

Similarly, metrics could have recorded (and did) the tonnage of the sheep and oxen sacrificed in Solomon's temple, but not what it was about them that made God say he was sick of them. In the same way, metrics can record the frequency of our church attendance, the regularity of our Bible reading and the exact amount of our tithing, but they can never gauge the genuineness of any of them, or whether they are any better than "the noise of the solemn assemblies" against which the prophets fulminated.

Or consider the trend toward numbers in the light of original sin. It should be obvious that any democratic people's "we" is just as corruptible, if not more so than any autocratic ruler's "I." It used to be called the "nostrism" of the many in contrast to the "egotism" of the one or the few, but it is no less corruptible. If we do not want mass democracy to degenerate into a new and subtle tyranny of King Demos and his regime of numbers, we must recognize and resist the trend. Legalization of any practice, and then its normalization through numbers, need never mean a revaluation of what we know to be wrong because God says so, simply because the majority opinion now holds it to be right. Ten million ignorant assertions, even when magnified and accelerated in a hundred million tweets and "likes," still never add up to truth or wisdom, or what is right and good.

What matters here, of course, is not the danger to democracy but to the church. We therefore need to trace the overall damage

of such worldly thinking. It develops Christians with an eye for
the quantitative rather than the qualitative, for externals rather
than inner reality, for performance rather than relationship, for
the shallow rather than the deep, for evangelism in terms of the
number of "decisions" rather than discipleship and growth in
character, for the bandwagon rather than the Bible, for popularity rather than principle, and with a greater sensitivity to
horizontal pressure than to vertical authority. Some Christians
have adopted a reverse of Mayor Bloomberg's position: "In
metrics we trust. All others must get by as best they can on their
trust in God." "Thus says the Lord" should always trump "51
percent now believe," but the current idolatry of metrics renders
Christians vulnerable to the mob-masters of the virtual age, the
high-tech wizards who can corral the opinion of millions within
minutes. (This is a crucial factor in the cataclysmic suddenness
of the triumph of the sexual revolution over the Jewish and
Christian faiths that have shaped Western civilization for two
thousand years.) The result is a church befuddled over the difference between success and faithfulness, hesitant to buck the
going trends, fearful to stick her neck out and find herself in the
minority, and reluctant to risk the loneliness of pursuing the true
and the excellent regardless of all outcomes—in short, a church
fatally weakened because worldly. In today's world, the courage
of Athanasius *contra mundum* would be scorned as Athanasius
marooned on the wrong side of history.

Doubtless, some will consider these comments ludicrous and
naive, for what could be more self-evident than our new science
of numbers? Admittedly, such forms of worldliness are subtle,
but whether they are subtle or crass, the goal of this friendly
caution is clear. The church of Christ across the Global South
must resist all worldliness, rise to its modern future with an
unalloyed and clear-eyed loyalty to Jesus and his kingdom, and

at the same time be prepared to engage with all the issues and challenges of advanced modernity, fully prepared and without fear. Will the future see the whole church of Christ both fully faithful and fully engaged in the modern world? Where the Western church once signally failed, the church in the Global South may yet succeed by the grace of God and so point the way forward for the Christian church as a whole.

WINNING BACK THE WEST

The second grand task for the worldwide church is to help win back the Western world to Jesus.

Let there be no misunderstanding. In a day of declining Western dominance, winning back the Western world to Jesus is not a matter of Western-centrism. As I said, I am not arguing on behalf of Western civilization. Nor am I nostalgic for a lost world, or sounding a call to any misguided culture-warring, as if politics were the answer to our decline. The sins of the West are all too clear. But what matters is that with the exception of God's chosen people Israel, all peoples, all generations, all cultures and all countries are equally near and dear to God's heart, so the West has no priority over any other culture.

The simple reason why we in the West have a duty to seek to win back the West is that it is our "Jerusalem," and every generation of followers of Jesus must begin to obey the Great Commission in their own Jerusalem as well as going out to the "uttermost parts of the earth." To Christians in the West, countries such as Korea and Kenya are the uttermost parts of the earth, just as we are the uttermost parts of the earth to them. But the West is our Jerusalem, our home base, the center of the concentric circles that make up our wider world. We are therefore called to go to our Jerusalem as well as to the uttermost parts of the earth.

Needless to say, such a mission would be the third mission

to the West, for we are the heirs of two earlier missions that have been decisive for our world. The first mission to the West centered on *the conversion of the Roman Empire*. This mission is well known, the extraordinary story of how those whom the Romans saw as a bunch of provincial misfits grew and grew until their faith replaced the faith of mighty Rome itself. (The Emperor Julian after his failure to turn back the clock: "You have conquered, Galilean!")

But when the Western Roman Empire fell in the fifth century, so also did much of the church in the West, so the second mission to the West centered on *the conversion of the barbarian kingdoms*.[15] This took place against the backdrop of the Dark Ages and the tribal conditions and conflicts from the fifth to the tenth centuries. Less well known than the story of the conversion of Rome, this story was every bit as heroic. It included the celebrated "gentling" of the European people, as the cross of Jesus became what the poet Heinrich Heine called the "taming talisman" that subdued the "berserker rage" of barbarians such as the Celts, the Goths, the Visigoths, the Franks and the Vikings.

The second mission also includes the stories of Skellig Michael and communities like it. Skellig Michael was the rocky pyramid in the storm-tossed Atlantic, eight miles off the western coast of Ireland. For six centuries, part of the church clung to its faith by the skin of its teeth at a place that for them was the end of the world and at a moment they believed was the end of time. The second mission certainly includes the story of "how the Irish saved civilization," the brief, bright hour captured by Thomas Cahill's book of the same title when St. Columbanus and other missionaries from the Emerald Isle fanned out down and across Europe, a missionary journey that can still be traced today by the trail of Celtic crosses as far down as St. Gallen in Switzerland and Bobbio in northern Italy.

What those of us who are European Christians must acknowledge humbly is that when the Chinese and other peoples in the world had reached a high level of civilization, we were still barbarians and we might still be barbarians apart from the gospel. It took the gospel of Jesus Christ to tame our barbarian violence and unite our warring continent. For the intrepid missionaries who sailed forth from Ireland in flimsy coracles, or who journeyed up from Rome under the second St. Augustine, brought both the gospel and its fruits. Along with the gospel, they brought the Scriptures, then literacy, then education, and all the gifts of the gospel that later on were to lay the foundations from which Christendom was built.

We have much to learn from both of these earlier missions to the West, but the point is that we stand in the dying light of the second mission whose great highlights over the centuries have included Christendom, the Reformation and the Great Awakenings. Our challenge is to shake ourselves free from the natural despondency of those who look only at circumstances and at the statistics of decline and gloom. (Like America itself, American Christians are slavish devotees of opinion polls and far too obsessed with statistics, when what matters are the "whys" and the "wherefores" rather than the "what.") The West has been won twice before, and now it appears that the West has almost been lost a second time. So now, partly in response to the courageous faith of those who achieved it twice before, but more in response to the Great Commission itself, it is time to set our minds and hearts to win back the West to our Lord again.

Pope Benedict issued a resounding call for the re-evangelization of the West, and many Evangelicals have long prayed and worked for the same goal. Can it be done? Can the West be re-won, not as a continuation of the present fruitless culture wars or as a new cultural crusade, but as a genuine re-evangelization and a powerful advance of the kingdom of God in the name of the Prince of Peace? The answer to that question will be the topic of the next chapters. What matters here is that we Western Christians, helped undoubtedly by our fellow Christians from across the world, must turn from the prevailing gloom and doom and set about the glorious task of winning back our societies and nations for our Lord.

Can Christians from both the West and the Global South so recover the integrity and effectiveness of faith that together we prevail against the challenges of modernity? There is no greater challenge than that, but equally there would be no greater hope for the world than that. With God nothing is impossible, but this is no time for idle dreams. The time has come to pray and act.

CONTRIBUTING TO THE HUMAN FUTURE

The third grand task for the worldwide church is to contribute constructively to the human future.

There is no doubt that modernity has already unleashed titanic challenges on the world, from the terrible human costs of industrialization, urbanization and consumerism to the savagery of total warfare in two great world wars and a Cold War. But we are about to enter a new era of even greater problems created by the many converging trends and forces of globalization.

Marshall McLuhan was famous for his description of the world as a "global village." But while the world is smaller in some ways, that picture is misleading in other ways and leaves an impression that is far too simple and cozy. In the globalizing world of today, the world is certainly smaller. We can see "everything as it happens," and we can "get anywhere from anywhere" in less than a day. But the world is also larger and more dangerous. With everything connected, and with a new awareness of the constant danger of risks, side effects and "unknown aftermaths," nothing is simple, limited and discrete any longer. Leaders of today's global world, such as presidents, prime ministers and CEOs, know well that they have to deal with "the whole world the whole time."

More seriously still, the last few generations have been the first in all history to have to contemplate soberly the real possibility of the destruction of the planet or the human destruction of the human race itself. Converging trends in economics, demography, technology, energy, the environment, morality and culture raise dilemmas that cannot be shrugged off.

To be sure, doom peddlers and false prophets will have their day, but the serious voices must never be lost amid the clamor. Lord Martin Rees was Britain's Astronomer Royal and Master of Trinity College, Cambridge, and certainly no alarmist. But in 2003 he warned soberly, "I think the odds are no better than fifty-fifty that our present civilization on Earth will survive to the end of the present century."[16] Oxford University futurist James Martin was equally blunt: "Even if *Homo sapiens* survives, civilization may not."[17]

Will Christians rise to play their part in responding to such challenges? No other faiths have rivaled the record of the Jewish and Christian faiths in facing up to evils and oppressions and launching recurring reforms in the name of God and justice. But the biggest global challenges of today and tomorrow may prove to be of an even greater magnitude. Tackling them will require an unshakable trust in God that can face any future without fear, a profound intellectual seriousness that is willing to wrestle with problems that are unprecedented in human experience, a constant reliance on God's Spirit for fresh and creative imagination to conceive of what has never yet been, and an untiring perseverance that will be worthy of the heroism of the greatest reformers of the past.

That is the formidable task to which the next generation of Christians must commit themselves. They will know that they are standing on the shoulders of the giants who have gone before—grateful for the prophet Amos and his stand on behalf of the poor, for Telemachus and his life given to end the horror of the gladiatorial games, for Bartolomé de las Casas and his outrage against the conquistadores for their treatment of the Native Americans, for William Wilberforce and his lifelong struggle to abolish slavery in the British Empire, for Lord Shaftesbury whose tireless compassion and industrial reforms made him the "poor man's Earl," for Florence Nightingale and her revolutionary contributions to the rise of modern nursing, for Martin Luther King Jr. and his costly triumph in the Civil Rights Movement, and for all the nameless host of Jewish and Christian social reformers whom they represent.

But standing on the shoulders of such giants, the coming generation of Christian men and women must tackle the even greater issues of the global era that otherwise threaten to call into question the very future of humanity and the planet itself. All that is certain is that there will be a myriad of such momentous global issues, and every passing year is likely to raise still more.

For many decades, my own concern has focused on a global issue that will lie beneath many of the other issues: how we are to live with our deepest differences, especially when those differences are religious and ideological, and most especially when they clash over matters of common public life. In short, how are we to forge a global public square?[18]

But that is only one such issue. Who will tackle a constructive Christian critique of capitalism, and its two most recent offspring, consumerism and financialization? Or end the nightmare of nuclear proliferation? Or ensure a just and reliable access to human essentials such as water? Or bridge the yawning inequities between the rich and poor, and the haves and the have-nots? Or model a rich and solid way of life for families and other institutions now melting down under the conditions of advanced modernity? Unquestionably, the list will go on and on, touching poverty, crime, disease and corruption, as well as less tangible realities such as meaning, hope and enterprise. But however long the list stretches, and however daunting its magnitude, followers of Jesus must be there and in the thick of things. When the great issues are clearer and their magnitude is evident, genuine rivals to the truth and adequacy of Christian visions and Christian solutions will turn out to be surprisingly few.

In sum, talk of a Christian renaissance in the West is not a parochial concern nor of limited interest only to the West. For any major world faith to be able to prevail against the pressures of advanced modernity, and then to have the capacity to bring constructive solutions to the problems of advanced modernity itself, is of world-historic significance. That, and no less, is the stake in any talk of a Christian renaissance in the West.

A Prayer

O God of Abraham, Isaac and Jacob, and of all who have gone before us on this earth, we give thanks for your faithfulness from generation to generation, and we ask your forgiveness that we live as if we were your only concern and our time were the only time there is. Grant that as we seek to serve you, we may understand our times, we may see our time in the light of all times and of eternity, and we may understand your purposes in our generation.

May no challenge or crisis daunt us, no enemy or attack unnerve us, and no failure or setback cause us to take our hands off the plough or let the sword slip from our hand. Grant then that we may rise to the challenges of our times as the great heroes of the faith did to theirs, so that together with them we may be the servant agents of your kingdom and worthy of your high calling. In the name of Jesus, Amen.

Questions for Discussion

1. In what ways are you and your local church in touch with the churches in the Global South? How do you think we can share with them our resources, but also say with humility, "Don't give in to the seductions and shaping of modernity as we have done"?

2. What difference would it make to view ourselves, not as in a dying situation, but as on a third mission to the West? What might this mean, and how would it be different from so much of today's culture warring?

3. What do you see as the greatest issues facing humanity in the future? Where does your individual calling engage with these issues? Where are the areas where there are few Christians, and where do we need to pray that God will raise up people to take them on?

3

UNNECESSARY, UNLIKELY, UNDENIABLE

There are many today who press the simple catchword "Jesus plus nothing." Followers of Jesus, they claim, should be concerned solely and simply with him. Everything else is beside the point and a potential doorway to worldliness. Not surprisingly, such people tend to be suspicious of any talk of the relationship between the Christian faith and culture. All such talk is likely to be worldly, they say, and a trap for the faithful to be avoided at all costs.

But the fact is, such piety is too pious by half. The intended compliment actually dishonors Jesus, and its advocates need to think more deeply. First, a literal interpretation of the maxim is overly simplistic. John Owen, the great seventeenth-century theologian of the cross, showed an equally faithful though less wooden interpretation. He quoted the apostle Paul's words to the Corinthians: "I have determined to know nothing but Jesus Christ and him crucified." But he then added: "At least with nothing that could divert my attention from that subject." Paul himself, of course, went on to speak of other things he also knew, including the details of the divisions in the church at Corinth and the facts of their sexual promiscuity.

Second, we could not know who Jesus is without going beyond Jesus. For a start, we would not understand Jesus and his life work without the entire Old Testament that preceded him. Indeed, it would be meaningless to bow to the staggering claims of Jesus without the unique revelations of God over the centuries. Take that away and Jesus could be just another avatar and not "Lord and God." Equally, we would not understand Jesus fully without the rest of the New Testament that followed him. As the disciples learned on the road to Emmaus, Jesus' own deepest explanation of his life and work could only be offered after his work had been done.

Third, the fact is that many who brandish this formula tend to teach only those parts of the teaching of Jesus that fit in with their own ideas. Like the many faulty "Jesuses" of Protestant liberalism, their teaching is merely a reflection of their own prejudices. Today's "Jesus plus nothing" had its forerunners in such maxims as "the fatherhood of God and the brotherhood of man." While sounding good, these formulae were not biblical and their effect was baneful.

Fourth, genuine seekers who are not simplistic and are searching for adequate answers will often conclude that those who have no interest in their wider questions will have no answers to the meaning of life. They therefore walk away from the presumed childishness of the Christian faith.

Fifth, it was Jesus who was concerned with far more than just himself, so to be faithful to him is to scrap the slogan, however well meaning. Indeed it is Jesus himself who raises the question of the Christian relationship to culture—for example, in his famous response "Render to Caesar what is Caesar's," or when he prays for his followers who are to remain "in" the world, but not "of" it. As his full teaching makes clear and the rest of the New Testament amplifies, "worldliness" and its opposite, "other-worldliness," are the two extremes that Christians are called to avoid, and the challenge is to follow him in the more faithful and far more demanding position in between. Far from un-faithful, as we shall see, this creative Christian engagement with culture and with the world is a key source of the power of the gospel in the church and of Christians in the world.

Lastly, the sad fact is that talk of "Jesus plus nothing" usually ends in holding to a form of Christian faith that is "Jesus minus something." Most often it represents a faith with an inadequate grasp of truth or too little theology and thought, or a faith that is "all Jesus" and no God the Father and no proper place for the Holy Spirit. With some who espouse this maxim, it has become a significant source of syncretism and unfaithfulness in the wider church.

That said, the caution about worldliness is a useful spur, espe-cially if it prompts us to think more deeply about Christian faith and culture, and to remember how the relationship between them is surprising, highly surprising, and needs to be attended to with great care. Let me underscore three points that grow out of that relationship.

UNNECESSARY

First, it is worth noting that the Christian faith is not necessary for either the making of culture or the building of civilization. It is a straightforward matter of observation that there are countless cultures without any faith in Jesus Christ, just as there have been many civilizations dedicated to numerous faiths that were any-thing but Christian. It is not part of our Christian argument that without faith in Jesus there could be no culture or civilization.

It is certainly arguable that apart from Jesus, no culture and no civilization could have certain qualities that are unique to him and his teaching. In that sense, Emil Brunner in his Gifford Lectures stated his firm conviction that "only Christianity is capable of furnishing the basis of a civilisation which can rightly be described as human."[1] It is also arguable, as Friedrich Nietzsche among others has argued, that there will be inevitable consequences if a society rejects the Christian faith that has been its inspiration and foundation. Both Greece and Rome withered from the inside, and so also will the West as it loses its animating faith. If, as Lord Acton stated, religion is the key to history, then a change in faith means a change in culture and a change in life—and far, far more than merely a change in thought.

But the point still stands that there have been many cultures and many civilizations that owed nothing to Jesus or to the Jewish and Christian Scriptures in any discernible way. Of what are often said to be the world's nine greatest cultures and civilizations—Egyptian, Babylonian, Indian, Chinese, Mayan, Grecian, Roman, Arabian and Western—only the last owes anything expressly to the Christian faith. Behind every civilization lies a vision and a worldview, and none is greater or more lasting than the strength of its vision.

By the same token, the great majority of humans might well agree on what are the basic questions confronting us as humans (the problem of reality, meaning, truth, purpose, time, evil, suffering, human worth, personality, justice, freedom and so on), but there is no agreement over the answers. Whatever answers human beings have reached have been put into many different frames and worldviews, and many would differ radically from the Jewish and Christian understanding.

This point runs parallel to the discussion of the common question, "Can someone be good without God?" Many atheists, such as Christopher Hitchens, have tried to make hay with the claim that you don't need God to be good, and that many people are good without God. Some Christians would deny their claim, but most would gladly recognize that many people are "good without God," and in the same way that many cultures and many civilizations have been "great without God."

On the one hand, there is the copious evidence of history and our daily lives. Who, for example, would deny the courage of Alexander the Great, the insatiable curiosity of Socrates, the brilliance of the creations of Leonardo da Vinci, or the countless admirable qualities that many of us recognize in our neighbors and colleagues? Equally, who would deny the greatness of Athens under Pericles, or Rome under Hadrian, or the Egypt of the Pharaohs, or the China of the Ming dynasty?

Further, there are strong theological reasons to underpin this recognition. "All truth is God's truth," as St. Augustine and other early Christian writers taught, for even when and where God is not acknowledged, the fabric of truth is one and indivisible, and its source is the God of truth. And whatever they believe, pagans and enemies of God included, all humans are made in the image of God and are therefore capable of being good, discovering truth, creating beauty and achieving greatness—whether they acknowledge God or not.

This means that regardless of whether cultures and civilizations acknowledge God, Christians who know God should be among the first to praise and be grateful for truth, for beauty, for goodness and for greatness wherever it may be found. The Christian should always remember, as St. Augustine wrote, "Wherever truth may be found it belongs to his Master."[2] Not for one moment am I arguing that without the Christian faith, there can be no culture or civilization, or—though this appears more likely—that Western culture will necessarily collapse completely if it rejects the Christian faith that has been its foundation.

CULTURE AND CIVILIZATION SIMPLY PUT

Before we go further, we must stop and ask what we mean by the terms *culture* and *civilization*, as both of them run through this book like a recurring thread. The two terms are often defined and explored in ways that are complicated and best left to scholars and specialists. But we can also define and use them in ways that are simple, accurate and highly relevant to our faith.

Take the first term. In essence, a *culture* is simply "a way of life lived in common." In that sense, we can talk of French, Hungarian or Chinese culture as the ways of life lived in France, Hungary and China, and among other things this would include the French taste for wine and cheese, the Hungarian love for folk music, and the Chinese respect for their families, for their ancestors and for tradition.

In the same way, we can talk of "youth culture" or "modern culture," and by the same token we can properly talk of "Christian culture." Jesus called and still calls his followers to himself as individuals, but followers of Jesus are never to remain simply individuals. For the Christian faith is not simply a personal faith, a worldview, a way of life, a creed, but a community and a society. This is too often forgotten in our modern individualistic societies. A key part of the primary call of each follower of Jesus is that we are commanded as his disciples *to live his way of life and to do so together*—which, when it is done, leads naturally to a "Christian culture," or a Christlike way of life lived in common by followers of Christ. As we live by faith, from our waking to our sleeping, from the first days of our conversion to the last, and from one end of our world to the other, that way of life is a culture in embryo, and when we live it with others, it becomes a full-grown culture.

It has been argued that there is no great or lasting culture without a religion, and that a culture is essentially the embodiment of a religion or a worldview—there is no culture without a cult. For example, T. S. Eliot believed that "no culture has appeared or developed except together with a religion."[3] Be that as it may, I am making the simpler point that a way of life lived in common creates a culture. We must therefore never minimize the natural and necessary link between the gospel and culture. Jesus underscored that his followers' way of life *lived together*—for example in their love for each other—was to be the demonstration of what he and his teaching meant: "A new commandment I give to you, that you love one another, even as I have loved you, that you also love one another. By this all men will know that you are My disciples, if you have love for one another."[4]

This means that the Christian faith must always be open to scrutiny on two levels: one concerning its credibility and the other concerning its plausibility. At the level of credibility, the Christian faith can be put under the microscope in terms of its truth claims. The question then is whether the claims of faith can be examined and found to be true, so that the believer's faith is truly credible as a warranted faith that is believed to be true and in accord with the reality of what finally *is*.

But there is another level at which it is the plausibility, rather than the credibility of faith, which is at stake. The question then is whether the Christian faith "appears to be true" because it is practiced consistently by those who believe and follow it—or whether we are rationalizing (giving reasons other than the real reasons) or, worse still, whether we are plain and simple hypocrites. At this level, the Christian life can be put under the microscope in terms of the consistency of its practitioners. Regardless of what we Christians say we believe, are we in fact "walking the talk" and practicing what we preach? The question

at this level is whether our Christian faith appears to be true to
the wider, watching world when judged by the fruit it produces
in the lives of ~~we~~ us who are its followers.

It would be a cardinal error to confuse the kingdom of God
with any human civilization, though this has been done too
often in history and there are examples of the same mistake
today. The kingdom of God is always higher and other than our
cultural life, but it does not divorce us from the cultures in
which we live. These considerations mean in turn that an appreciation of "Christian culture" is vital for at least two reasons
(the term *Christian culture* simply being another way of saying
"the way of Jesus lived in common").

First, an appreciation of Christian culture is vital because it is a
direct indication of the social impact of Christian faithfulness. If
Christians are living as "salt and light" in any society, and they reach
a critical mass where they are more than a small counterculture,
then the "Christianness" or otherwise of that society (the degree to
which that society reflects the way of Jesus) is a test of the degree
to which Christians are living out the way of Jesus in obedience.

A striking symptom of the church's problems in the West
today is the fact that in a country such as the United States,
Christians are still the overwhelming majority of citizens, but
the American way of life has moved far from the way of life of
Jesus—which means simply that the Christians who are the majority are living a way of life closer to the world than to the way
of Jesus. In a word, they are worldly and therefore incapable of
shaping their culture.

Second, an appreciation of Christian culture is vital because
it is a direct measure of the plausibility of the Christian faith to
others in any society. The same "Christianness" of the society
(the degree to which the society truly reflects the way of Jesus)
will be a demonstration to the wider world of the plausibility of

Christian faith at any moment in time.

To the degree that Christians are living the way of Jesus faithfully and in common, to that degree it can be said that there is a hope of a substantially Christlike culture, and to that degree the Christian faith will also be plausible in society. Many Christians are skeptical of this today. Seeing only the widespread corruptions of the church around them, they despair of such cultural change happening at anything higher than a personal or local level. But this is to restrict the power of God to the dismal levels of our expectations of our world today. To be sure, consistent Christian living may be harder the higher it reaches, but this is no excuse for mediocre expectations and standards.

Conversely, of course, to the degree that we Christians are not practicing what we preach, we cannot expect our society to enjoy the fruits of the way of life of Jesus, and our Christian faith is likely to be implausible and off-putting to the wider world. In sum, the questions of culture are important for faith because they are a vital indicator of how we are living out our faith together in practice.

We need to ponder just how challenging this task is today. Over the last generations, different waves of radical talk have passed through many Evangelical churches, each wave bringing a new energy and excitement as it appears to offer a real remedy for the church's very real malaise. But has the net effect been the creation of a more distinctively Christian culture or wider social impact?

Not so far. On the one hand, a genuine counterculture, which is a way of life lived in common that is truly different from the world is far from easy and straightforward. It is against the grain of the advanced modern world, and one of the hardest and costliest things to achieve in our time-pressured, highly mobile, strung-out, open, advanced modern societies. Besides, most forms of the new Christian radicalism have been served up in the old late-twentieth century, worldly promotion style—with the roving spotlight picking out the latest bestselling celebrity authors du jour, oversold conferences, and the aura of the fastest growing megachurches of the moment—though with the rising cost of travel and the sinking readership of books, the twenty-first century equivalent may be the number of "likes" on Facebook and the number of "followers" on Twitter.

Worse still, the problem is aggravated by the fact that, despite distinguished current exceptions, some of the so-called radicalism is actually a shrunken version of faith, which is deficient in theology, unaware of history and lacking a robust understanding of calling—and therefore incapable of truly engaging society and creating culture. Similarly, much radical talk has turned into radical chic, and then disappeared as one more passing spasm in the life of the churches—whose members never notice as they rush toward the "new person of the hour" whom the media has anointed to replace the last one.

In strong contrast, culture creation requires a long obedience over several generations, which requires a steady engagement with wider society through the callings of all believers in all their lives, which requires strong, stable lives lived in common, which requires a vibrant worshiping, teaching and fellowshiping community, which requires a faith that is true to Jesus above all rival claimants such as personal lifestyle, political party, economic imperatives and entertainment fashions.

In short, we must foster a robust discipleship with a faith worthy of our Lord—with a reach as high as the awe and majesty of God, as deep as the depths of the Scriptures, as rich as the stories and lessons of history, and as wide as the infinite varieties of the worldwide church. Unquestionably, culture creation requires time and perseverance. It is not a matter of harvesting mushrooms but of growing oak trees.

What do we mean by the second term, *civilization*? Once

again, the term can be defined in complicated ways, but in essence a civilization can be defined simply as "a culture with sufficient extension, duration and elevation." That is to say, the idea of civilization is closely linked to the idea of culture, for a civilization is a culture that has reached a certain stage of expansion and advance.

More precisely, a civilization is a culture that spreads widely enough (sufficient extension), that lasts long enough (sufficient duration), and above all that rises high enough to merit the praise of later generations (sufficient elevation)—whether for the excellence of its arts, its science, its technology, its prowess in military conquest, or in some other area of human achievement. The culture of Athens, for example, stretched back centuries before Pericles, but it was in the generation of the great statesman that it flowered riotously into the immortal glory that was Greek civilization in its golden age.

Needless to say, there is a paradox in what we are discussing. On the one hand, I am not defending the "Christian West" or suggesting that we should ever make "Christian culture" or "Christian civilization" our goal. All Christian cultures will be flawed like the Christians who create them, and as we shall see, our aim should always be to advance the kingdom of God rather than create culture. But on the other hand, Christian faithfulness will always have cultural consequences, if only as a by-product of Christians following the call of Jesus and aiming for higher and other things.

UNLIKELY

But what on earth has the way of Jesus to do with Greece, or Rome, or Egypt, or Babylon, or Persia, or China? In the logic of Tertullian's famous question that has echoed down the centuries, "What indeed has Athens to do with Jerusalem?"[5] Surely there is no contradiction in all history greater than the chasm between

Jesus and the great captains of history, or between the church and the empires of the world.

The much-quoted lines at the heart of "One Solitary Life" captured well the sheer improbability of Jesus of Nazareth being the inspiration for culture and civilization. "He never wrote a book. He never held an office. He never had a family or owned a house. He didn't go to college. He never visited a big city. He never traveled two hundred miles from the place where he was born. He did none of those things one usually associates with greatness."[6]

What were the odds that a rural carpenter's son from an obscure backwater of the Roman Empire would outshine the pride and glory of the greatest emperor and the mightiest warrior captains of history? How likely was it that the birthday of a man viewed as a disgraced and executed provincial criminal would come to mark the year that for most of the world divides all history? As Christopher Dawson noted, from the perspective of a secular historian the life of Jesus "was not only unimportant, but actually invisible."[7]

And yet. And yet.

The truth is that Tertullian's question was not as simplistic and obscurantist as it is often suggested, and the relationship of Jesus and culture is not as black or white as the choice is so often presented. But there is no question about the improbability, and this improbability is not accidental. The way of Jesus is dramatically different from the way of the world. The relationship of Jesus to the great civilizations of history is highly unlikely, and the reasons for it must always be respected and must never be lost.

Our Lord openly declares to his critics in the Gospel of John, "You are of this world, I am not of this world."[8] Ten chapters later, in answer to Governor Pontius Pilate as he is tried for his life, he declares with the same unequivocal clarity, "My kingdom is not of this world. If My kingdom were of this world, then My servants would be fighting so that I would not be handed over to the Jews; but as it is, My kingdom is not of this realm."[9]

The same story line runs through the whole account of the life and work of Jesus. He flatly refused the temptations of power and fame offered him by the Grand Inquisitor from hell. He was no Judas Maccabeus *redevivus*. His conspiracy was not that of the Zealots of his day. His revolutionary manifesto was not a bloody call to arms like that of Marx and Engels, Hitler and Himmler, Mao Zedong and Pol Pot. His mission was not at the point of a sword like Muhammad's. In fact, Jesus was the unarmed prophet who renounced the sword, and seemed to turn away from the use of force that any civilization needs in order to build and sustain itself. And he appeared to show little or no interest in many of the burning issues that parade across our television screens, shout at us in the headlines of our newspapers, and rage like wildfire through our social media.

How then could such a master, so emphatically and staggeringly different, ever be connected with the making of culture or the building of a civilization and a worldly empire? It is beyond improbable. It must surely be unthinkable. As Brunner sums it up,

> Anyone who approaches the New Testament with the intention of getting instruction about the relation between Christian faith or doctrine and civilisation or culture from the most authoritative source, cannot fail to be astonished, bewildered, and even disappointed. Neither the Gospels nor the letters of the apostles, neither the teaching of Jesus himself, nor that of his disciples, seem to encourage us in any way to investigate this relation.[10]

And yet, and yet.

While all the above is true, it is also arguable that the Christian faith has been the decisive factor in the creation of what may be the most powerful civilization the world has ever seen. All empires and civilizations in history so far have been regional and therefore limited in terms of territory as well as time. Even Rome, for all the immense size of its empire and its boasts about being the "eternal city" and the *caput mundi* ("head of the world"), was still a regional empire that never conquered India, China, most of Africa, the Americas—or even Ireland and Scotland.

Yet in contrast to these earlier empires, a central feature of our advanced modern global civilization is that it may become truly global and not regional. Its dynamism, coming from the combined forces of science, capitalism and technology, is nothing short of global in its potential and its pretensions, and the civilization that it produces may well be truly global and on a scale that dwarfs all the regional superpowers that have come and gone before.

But how is that attributable to Jesus and the Christian faith, even indirectly? After all, the Western world is surely the product of the pre-Christian civilizations that preceded it. To be sure, the West owes a vast debt to the Greeks, the Roman and the Jews. Among the gifts we owe to the first are our philosophy, our science, our political understanding, our drama and our sculpture. Among the gifts we owe to the second are our understanding of the art of power, government, law, order, and the importance of such communications as roads and such conveniences as warm baths and central heating. (Virgil: "Romans, keep in mind that your art form is government."[11]) And among the gifts we owe to the third are our belief in human dignity and freedom, our sense of history and human agency, our high valuation of ethics and responsibility, and the strength of our millennia-long commitment to heterosexual marriage and the primacy of the family as the bedrock of society.

Yet true though that acknowledgment is, a moment's thought would remind us that all three of these civilizations were Mediterranean, whereas the West is far more than Mediterranean. It is

European, American, Canadian, Australian and now far beyond. The point is that for all the gifts of the preceding civilizations, what made the West the West was Christian faith, for it was not only Julius Caesar's conquest of Gaul but the conversion of the barbarian kingdoms of Europe to Christ that laid the foundations for what was to become the West. It was only when the savage, warring tribes were gentled by the power of the cross that the barbarians could become peaceful. It was only when the light of the gospel lit up the rocky outcrop at the western end of the great Asian landmass that the civilization was founded that first became known as "Christendom," then "Europe," and later "the West." Both "Europe" and "the West" have always had a cultural meaning that goes beyond the geographical. They are about ideas and values, projects, dreams and visions, rather than simply places on a map.

Christian faith made the West? If not true, absurd, it might be said. The improbability of those first two missions alone—the conversion of Rome and the conversion of the barbarian kingdoms—is enough to underscore the unlikelihood of the way of Jesus ever producing culture and civilization. Yet it is a plain fact of history that both the famous Roman sword and the fearsome barbarian axe and club were all laid at the feet of the unarmed Prince of Peace whose followers were the real creators of the West.

UNDENIABLE

Today, we are living in the twilight of the Western world when, as in previous declining cultures, it is fashionable for the sophisticated and the couth to turn against the "old faith" that once inspired and empowered the former greatness. Ours is therefore an ABC moment ("Anything but Christianity"). For one thing, we are told tirelessly that "religion poisons everything" and given the impression that such evils as the Crusades and the

Inquisition are the characteristic, almost the sum total of, Christian contributions to Western history. For another, the legacy of postcolonialism and its general requirement of guilt feelings and breast-beating mean that we have been made to feel bad about all the distinctive features of our culture and civilization. The Christian contributions were curses, not gifts, we are told. They are what is wrong with the world.

There was certainly much to confess in Western history. But critics such as the new atheists show such lack of discrimination and such foolish and ill-tempered ignorance as to do them no credit. This in turn serves to blind the eyes and dull the ears of their audiences to the real history of the West and to the crucial questions of the relationship of the best of the past to the challenges of the present. We must certainly confess the sins we have committed and, as I keep insisting, I am arguing for the Christian faith and not for the West itself. But it is no casual matter for any generation to sever the roots of its culture, for nothing is more certain than the fact that cut-flower civilizations cannot and will not last.

What if Jesus had never been born? Many serious speculations have pondered that question. More specifically, what are the distinctive features of the West that are the direct gifts of the Christian faith? Vigorous and lengthy answers have been given to this topic. See, for example, Rodney Stark's *The Rise of Christianity*. I will briefly mention only the following five salient contributions.

First, the West has a strong tradition of philanthropy that has created a culture of giving and caring that is unmatched in any other civilization in history. The parable of the good Samaritan has by itself been described as "the parable that changed the world." But along with such specific teaching, the first century witnessed a historic convergence of Jewish and Christian answers to the foundational questions, "Money: Whose is it?" "Giving: Why do it?" and "Caring: Who should I care for?"

In each case, the answers differed decisively from both the Greek and Roman answers of the day, and from the answers of the other major world religions. It was the explosion created by these combined answers that was the dynamic thrust behind the rise of Western hospitals, orphanages, leprosariums and the hospices for the dying. For those who followed Jesus, the poor, the sick, the homeless, the prisoner, the unemployed, the stranger and the dying were the focus of the love of God and therefore of human care. To ignore this contribution or to hamper its proponents today, as several governments are trying to do, is to kill the goose that laid the golden egg.

Second, the West has a blood-red tradition of recurring reform movements that has no parallel in other civilizations. I mentioned some of the best-known heroes earlier, such as Las Casas and Wilberforce, but behind them are such giants as Roger Williams fighting for religious freedom for all, Elizabeth Fry reforming prisons, Dietrich Bonhoeffer resisting the evils of Nazism, Gary Haugen freeing prisoners from modern sex trafficking and bonded slavery today, and countless other names who fought against the evils of their day and dared to believe that a better world was possible. And here too the contrast with other faiths is strong. Hinduism, for example, has no such tradition, and the rise of native Indian reformers owed everything to the challenge posed by Christian missionaries and reformers such as William Carey.

Third, the West is the source of the universities that today represent one of the most powerful institutions of the modern world. Some have traced their origin back to Plato's Academy or to the madrasa at Cairo's Al-Azhar Mosque, but there is no doubt that the immediate and more powerful source behind the first universities in Bologna, the Sorbonne, Oxford and Cambridge was the rise of the cathedral schools in the late medieval world. One has only to look at their mottoes. Oxford's, for example, is the opening words of Psalm 27, *Dominus Illuminatio Mea* ("The Lord is my light").

Fourth, the West is the fountainhead of modern science, which along with capitalism and technology is revolutionizing the global world. To be sure, the roots of science go back to the insatiable curiosity of the Greeks, and owe much to its preservation and continuation in the Muslim era. But as many scholars such Alfred North Whitehead have argued, the matrix of modern science was a fruit of the Reformation and its worldview. Equally, the so-called "war between science and religion" is a nineteenth-century fiction created by secularists such as Andrew Dickson White, cofounder of Cornell University, which has now been discredited by serious historians.

Fifth, the West is the pioneer and champion of human dignity, human rights and the entire human rights revolution—all of which owes its origin to the Jewish and Christian understanding of men and women made "in the image of God." In today's world, the foundations and the universality of human rights are under assault from secularists on one side and from many religions on the other, so that human rights are dismissed as "Western particularism" and "Eurocentrism." But such attacks only serve to highlight how true it is that the roots of human rights cannot be traced back to other religions and ideologies, and they long preceded the Enlightenment. If in this case, as in others, the Christian faith served as what Benjamin Disraeli described as "Judaism for the multitudes," the point is still clear. Human dignity and human rights are the gifts to the world of the Jewish and Christian faiths.

Where does this leave us? This chapter is only a cursory glance at the issue, but it is enough to establish the point. With due respect for the atheist critiques of the church's evils, it is arrant nonsense for Christopher Hitchens to claim that "religion poisons everything." With full integrity, we can say with theologian John Baillie, "The historical permeation of our society by

Christian ideas and ideals is a development for which we must be profoundly grateful to the Lord of all history."[12]

In sum, the Christian faith has a highly unlikely and improbable relationship to culture and civilization, yet it is one that is also undeniably strong and unbreakable. Such a relationship will always be mercurial, and it is likely to prove ever-changing as it morphs from generation to generation and society to society. It must therefore never be stated or pursued in ways that are fixed or wooden, and it must always be understood and respected in terms of its own dynamics. It is to a key part of these dynamics that we turn next.

A Prayer

O Lord, great Creator of our great universe and all its splendors, and lover of all that is true and good and beautiful, we give thanks for all your works and for your giving us the privilege of being creators too under you. Forgive us that, made in your image, we have represented you so poorly, and we have been such irresponsible stewards in the world that you gave us to order and to enjoy. Grant that even now we may become such faithful agents of your kingdom and entrepreneurs of your calling, that the fruit of your gifts, and the schemes of our minds and the works of our hands may once again produce a way of life that is true to our calling and worthy to represent you. In the name of Jesus, Amen.

Questions for Discussion

1. How would you express a biblical view of the relationship of faith in Jesus to engagement in culture? Is such a view common among the Christians you know?

2. What are some of the mistaken views of faith and culture that block such a fruitful relationship?

3. What would the Western world be like if Jesus had never been born? What might it look like in the future if it rejects all Christian truths, and does so knowingly in a deliberate denial and contradiction of its own past?

4

THE SECRET OF
CULTURAL POWER

Dare we ask what is the secret of the cultural power of the Christian faith? There are enemies of the church who take great pleasure in pronouncing that the church has no power at all today, and who then go on to do all they can to ensure that the situation stays that way. Equally there are Christians who fear that all power is corrupt, and therefore resist any mention of power as a worldly exercise that will result in some new Constantinian compromise and a betrayal of the gospel.

There are still other Christians who would say that the very question sets off a misguided quest. The only answer we should give to the question of the secret of the church's cultural power is that the Christian faith is true, and that its power is the power of God himself. We should say nothing less, these critics say, and certainly nothing more. Seen this way, nothing else matters, no other factors count, and to attribute the cultural power of the church to anything else will take away the credit due solely to the Lord and will eventually lead us to the hubris and folly of self-reliance.

In short, these critics say, if the Christian faith is true, and
God is God, as we affirm, then we need not look for any explanation beyond the fact that God works in power through his
people, who with his help make a difference in the world of their
time and thus change culture in their turn. God is the one who
does it, God and God alone. That is the beginning and the end
of the matter and all we need to say.

Yet once again, this attitude is too pious by half. The power of
God through the Spirit of God is unquestionably the deepest
source of all true change, whether of people or cultures. Because
of the Word of God, through whom the universe itself sprang
into being, and because of the Spirit of God, who moves like the
wind to create and to sustain, we can affirm with confidence that
no change is impossible, no resistance is immovable, and no
possible futures are beyond our reach. By faith we can remove
mountains, and our first, last and greatest contribution is our
trust in the One who does what matters and does what it takes.

God's power is beyond question, and our full and final trust
must always be in the Word and the Spirit, the whole Word and
the Spirit, and nothing less than the Word and the Spirit. It is
also true that there are times in all our lives when it is absolutely
plain that God does everything, and we do nothing—and we
know that is so, beyond a shadow of doubt, because our human
resources are meager or nonexistent.

But is that all we can say, and is that true for the whole of
life—that God does everything and we do nothing? Of course
not, and we are free to ask how Christian faithfulness and obedience play their part in the grand partnership of God's sovereignty and human significance—in our engagement with culture
just as in the rest of our lives.

The truth is, the power of God through his Spirit is always the
all-decisive factor, and faith rests confidently in that final fact.

But such is the character and the cultural shape of Christian truth that the practice of that truth carries enormous power too. In other words, *when followers of Jesus live out the gospel in the world, as we are called to do, we become an incarnation of the truth of the gospel and an expression of the character and shape of its truth. It is this living-in-truth that proves culturally powerful.* It is therefore entirely legitimate to inquire into how Christian faithfulness and obedience to the truth serve the purposes and the power of God to change the world.

What do I mean by "the character and shape of truth"? Following Richard Weaver, it has become commonplace to say that "ideas have consequences," in the sense that certain consequences follow logically from certain assumptions. But too often this observation is left at the logical and theoretical level only. Individual ideas certainly have a logic of their own, but when ideas are linked together and framed as a set of ideas, as in a worldview, and when they are lived out in conjunction with others, they form an even stronger character and social shape. Such ideas have inevitable cultural consequences. In other words, a critical mass of believers consistently living out the shape of a set of ideas in a culture will always have an impact on the culture—for better or worse and in one way or another.

In short, if ideas have consequences, if differences make a difference, and if beliefs shape behaviors, how much more so do worldviews and ways of life when lived out powerfully in the cultures they are shaping. Anyone observing an aboriginal habitat in Australia, a Buddhist monastery in Thailand, a Marxist political congress in China, or a secularized modern suburb in Southern California can easily trace the links between the different views of the world and the different ways of life that they embody.

How much more so is that true of the Christian faith, which has the infinitely supercharged power of its being true. The way

of Jesus as "a life lived in common" will always be enormously
powerful in its impact on culture. As we saw, it has shaped many
societies and even created a great civilization.

BLESSEDLY TWO-EDGED

Various writers have quarried different aspects of this link between the characteristic shape of Christian truth and the resulting
shape of the culture it produces. Some have dug deep and mined
the point extensively, while others have made passing comments
that reveal their awareness of this insight. In the process, whether
it was their purpose or not, they served to highlight the secret of
the culture-shaping power of the Christian faith.

One example is C. S. Lewis's essay "Some Thoughts," in
which he argues that the Christian faith is highly distinctive
among religions and worldviews for being both "world-affirming"
and "world-denying" at the same time. At the heart of the
Christian faith, he writes, is the "undying paradox" of its
"blessedly two-edged character."[1] This feature grows directly
from the twin doctrines of creation and fall, and when lived out
in practice, gives the church a characteristic social and cultural
shape that makes its distinctive mark on culture.

Some religions and worldviews, such as ancient Confucianism
and modern secularism, are characteristically world affirming.
They unashamedly affirm the importance of the world "under
the sun," and of life here and now. That is not surprising, because the adherents of such worldviews believe only in this
world and have no comprehension of anyone or anything that
is other, higher or beyond this world. In Max Weber's famous
term, such secularists are "tone deaf" to other realities. They do
not hear the music by which most humans understand the universe and orchestrate their lives. In Peter Berger's equally famous
picture, they live in "a world without windows."[2] Reality, as they

view it, is all this side of the ceiling and the walls. In contrast to those worldviews that regard the unseen as more real than the seen, they believe only what they can see and have access to through the five senses. What is unseen is also unreal.

In direct contrast, Lewis argues, there are other religions and worldviews, such as Buddhism and gnosticism, which are characteristically world denying. Indeed, Buddhism has been described as the most gigantic "No" ever addressed to human aspirations in this world. All that we think we know of reality here and now is actually an illusion (*maya*), and the only way to achieve freedom is to escape this world of illusion and gain a measure of right-mindfulness en route to discovering the "not-self" and reaching *nirvana*, the great deathless lake of extinction.

Which side does the Christian faith favor? Does it affirm the world or deny it? Lewis argues that there is no point in asking on which side of the ledger you should put the Christian faith, because it insists squarely on being on both sides. In line with the strong biblical view of creation, pronounced by God as "good" and "very good," the Christian faith celebrates life and all the cornucopia of gifts given to us by God as blessings in our human lives. It affirms the secular without being secularist. It delights in the this-worldly without being worldly. It glories in all created life under God.

So the Christian church survived the fall of the Roman Empire, Lewis wrote, and became the agent that preserved what remained of secular civilization—"civilized agriculture, architecture, laws, and literacy itself."[3] Since then, Christians have gone on to make distinguished contributions to art, music, drama, sculpture, writing, and all the avenues by which knowledge can be pursued and beauty portrayed. And Christians also glory in the simple gifts of God, such as the sun, the wind, the rain, the snow and the seasons, and all the joys of daily life, including families, friends, comradeship, food, wine, sex, sports and a thousand other pleasures. Consider the exuberant gratitude for nature, for Brother Sun and Sister Moon and all our fellow creatures in St. Francis's "Canticle of the Sun."

But in line with the Bible's equally strong view of the fall and the effects of sin, the Christian faith is unashamed to glory in the cross as well as creation, to teach the place of Lenten fasting as well as Christmas feasting, the importance of sacrifice and not just fulfillment, and the hope of another world as well as joy in this one.

It is true that, sinners as we are, we Christians often lose our natural sense of spiritual balance. Many Christians down the ages have ignored the biblical balance and veered toward one extreme or the other. Some, as in prosperous times like ours, have become highly worldly, and others, in darker and more straightened circumstances, have verged on what Lewis called a "disdain for the whole natural order" and even justified a contempt for the world as a Christian virtue.[4]

Regrettable though these extremes are, what matters is that the Christian faith itself contains a wholeness that is profound and striking. So when the priority of faith is restored, it always serves to right the imbalance and return the church to the harmony and wholeness of the gospel. Once again, it is the social and cultural shape of Christian truth that realigns our living-in-truth and is therefore decisive in the end.

CONTRAST IS THE MOTHER OF CLARITY

Another less-known example is David Martin's contrast between the Christian faith and Marxism—which contrary to many Western impressions is still very much alive in certain regions of the world, and will remain so while it stays the official ideology of the world's most populous nation. Writing in the 1970s, the eminent English sociologist addressed a situation where Marxism was still feared as the powerful alternative to the West and to democratic freedom, and most observers thought the prospects for the church were bleak, especially in Western Europe and most especially among the educated elites. Matthew Arnold's "Dover Beach" was all the rage, and the constant talk was of the "melancholy, long, withdrawing roar" of the "Sea of Faith" on the modern shore.[5]

Martin, however, always had the courage to take on the prevailing consensus of the day. Earlier he had been the first to mount a comprehensive critique of the long dominant secularization theory that equated the advance of modernity with the decline of religion. In his comparison of the church and Marxism, he was prepared to buck fashionable opinion about the church because he had long reflected on the social shape of the two competing truth claims and worldviews. At the time, the church looked in dire straits, whereas Marxism looked strong and confident, but Martin saw that the opposite was the case. However strong Marxism appeared, and however weak the church looked, Marxism in fact lacked two things that the church possessed, which in the end would mean the renewal of the church and the demise of Marxism. Needless to say, his contrast can be applied to ideologies other than communism.

Martin expressed his criticism of Marxism with a penetrating accuracy. "It is a paradox that the system which claimed that the beginning of all criticism was the criticism of religion should have ended up with a form of religion which was the end of criticism."[6]

Why was this so? On the one hand, Martin argued that Marxism lacked, and the church possessed, "a doctrine of its own failure," which could be the source of its ongoing self-criticism and renewal.[7] Marxism and the Communist Party in particular could never admit that they were wrong, so they rationalized evil after evil in both the Soviet Union and China, and in other places such as Cambodia, until the spreading cancer of their unacknowledged crimes and lies appalled all but their most die-hard believers.

The point is not that the Christian church has had cleaner hands than the Communist Party. Far from it. The church down the ages has committed appalling evils too—for example, the horror of the medieval pogroms against the Jews or of the sexual abuse scandals of the clergy today. But the crucial difference is that the Christian faith allows no evasions or equivocations. Sin is sin is sin is sin, and there is no way around it. Sin is no less sin when Christians commit it, and before God there are no two ways about sin, lies, evil, oppression and hypocrisy. They are wrong, wrong always and wrong everywhere. God judges and condemns both sin and sins, so they always require confronting, and this has blunt consequences for those who believe such a truth.

First, the "doctrine of their own failure" means that Christians are realistic about human fallibility. We all often go wrong—Christians and Christian leaders included. So human evil is always a possibility and never a surprise. We expect it, we watch out for it, and whenever we can, we guard against it, as in the notion of political checks and balances. If we admit that all of us can always go wrong, it is still challenging but far less difficult to face the fact that we have done it again.

And second, the Christian faith calls for an open and voluntary confession of our wrongs, whenever we are wrong. This too is challenging and it may certainly be embarrassing for anyone who has to do it, but it is in fact an act of moral courage. For in confession we are called to do what no human does naturally and easily: to go on record against ourselves.

On the other hand, Martin argued that Marxism lacked, and the church possessed, "a judgment that transcended history."[8] It is a dogma of Marxism that the Communist Party is the incarnation of the will of history. In practice, this meant that the so-called will of history was made subject to the anything-but-infallible whims and foibles of the stubborn old men in the Kremlin. In the end, of course, it meant that history moved on and left behind the old men in the Kremlin who had foolishly presumed to be its mouthpiece. No human voice can claim a monopoly, let alone claim to be infallible as a voice and a verdict on history—not the Kremlin, and certainly not the *vox populi* of Western social trends today

For the Soviets, that critical deficiency of Marxism received its comeuppance in 1989. For the Communist party in China, that day is still to come, but when it does, as it surely will, the reason will be the same. Marxism cannot admit its own failures and it has no authority higher than itself. It is therefore incapable of self-criticism and renewal.

Again, it would be nonsense to pretend that the Christian church has always had a better record, and history shows how nothing is more corrupting than the claim to the mantle of infallibility by any human leader. Lord Acton, who was a devout Catholic layman but a lover of freedom, remarked acidly when he heard of the cardinals voting for papal infallibility in 1870, "They went in as shepherds, and they came out as sheep."

For the church, the judgment that transcends history is the Word of God inspired by the Spirit of God, spoken in Jesus through the Holy Spirit and now speaking in the Scriptures. Again, what is all-decisive is the Word, the whole Word and nothing less than the Word. To be sure, the church's understanding of the Word and Spirit of God is always shaped in part by the culture of its time, and is sometimes fatally distorted by that culture. But the Word and the Spirit of God are themselves above all cultures, so when they speak with their own divine

authority, they can break into culture irresistibly and penetrate
the culture-blindness and the culture-bound captivity of the
church at its worst. They can make even the tone deaf to hear
and the culturally dead to awake.

It is that supreme power and authority of the Word of God—
powerful, objective and standing above the flux and flow of
history and human culture—which is the true source of Christian
self-criticism and the true hope of ongoing Christian renewal.
This is also the wellspring behind G. K. Chesterton's witty hope
that was mentioned at the beginning of the book: "At least five
times . . . the Faith has to all appearances gone to the dogs. In
each of these five cases, it was the dog that died."[9]

THE CITY OF GOD AND THE CITY OF THIS WORLD

The deepest and most comprehensive exposition of the place
and the power of the church in culture is St. Augustine's *City of
God*. In A.D. 410, Alaric and his Visigoths had sacked Rome, and
the event sent shockwaves around the civilized world. The fall
of the "eternal city" was a fall beyond belief, and a raging argument broke out between Christians and pagans as to who or
what was to blame for the disaster. Were the pagans right that
the gods abandoned Rome because the Romans had abandoned
the gods—for the one true God of the Christians? Had Romans
lost their patriotism and their allegiance to Rome because they
now put God above Caesar? Or was it that Christians, with their
ethic of love and forgiveness, were simply too soft to be the
rulers of a vast and sprawling empire that required stern and
often brutal control?

Three years later Augustine decided to enter the debate, and
in 413 he set out to offer his own answer, *The City of God*, which
took him a decade or more to complete and became his *magnum
opus*. The first ten books refuted the pagan charges with a series

of powerful but somewhat predictable replies. But in the later books, he reflected more deeply on the human story, and set his grand vision of history and his theory of the two cities: the City of God and the City of Man.

At the heart of humanity are two humanities of the heart: those with a love of self and a heart dedicated to themselves, and those with a love of God and a heart dedicated to God. From these two hearts grow two humanities, two ways of life and eventually two cities: the City of God, which is the heavenly city, typified by Jerusalem, and the City of Man, which is the earthly city, typified earlier by Babylon and then by Rome.

What is of decisive importance is the relationship between the two cities. Here and now, and in the short term, they are intermingled, indistinguishable and often hard to tell apart. But starting from quite different origins and leading to quite different destinations, they are mutually exclusive and utterly and completely different in the long term. Christian allegiance is therefore to the heavenly city, not the earthly. As citizens of the City of God, we are merely sojourners on earth and therefore never more than "resident aliens" in the City of This World.

What Augustine's earlier classic *Confessions* was to the individual seeker the journey of faith toward personal fulfillment in God—his *City of God* was to nations and to the course of history—the path toward the kingdom of God and a world of peace, justice and shalom. Just as individuals must decide what is true and what is to be their view of the world and their way of life, so individuals must decide whether they give their allegiance to the worldly city or to the heavenly city.

Augustine's vision of the two cities and their relationship ties in powerfully with both the understanding of Jesus and the recurring biblical theme of the relationship between those who are faithful to God and the world in which they live. As Jesus says in his prayer to his Father in the garden of Gethsemane, his followers are to be "in" the world, but "not of" the world.[10] St. Paul captures the same tension in his famous challenge to the Christians in Rome. Do not be "conformed," but "transformed" through the renewal of your minds.[11] For the early church, this tension was prefigured in the Exodus. The Israelites were to "plunder the Egyptian gold," but they were not to set up a "golden calf."[12] In the more recent words of the Hartford Declaration in 1975, Christians are called to be "against the world, for the world."

What we have here in the teaching of Jesus and the Scriptures, and amplified in Augustine, is the very heart of the secret of the culture-shaping power of the gospel in the church. When the church goes to either of two extremes, and is so "in the world" that it is of the world and worldly, or so "not of the world" that it is otherworldly and might as well be out of the world altogether, it is powerless and utterly irrelevant. But when the church, through its faithfulness and its discernment of the times, lives truly "in" but "not of" the world, and is therefore the City of God engaging the City of Man, it touches off the secret of its culture-shaping power. *For the intellectual and social tension of being "in" but "not of" the world provides the engagement-with-critical-distance that is the source of the church's culture-shaping power.*

In short, the decisive power is always God's, through his Word and Spirit. But on her side the church contributes three distinct human factors to the equation: engagement, discernment and refusal. First, the church is called to engage and to stay engaged, to be faithful and obedient in that it puts aside all other preferences of its own and engages purposefully with the world as its Lord commands. Second, the church is called to discern, to exercise its spiritual and cultural discernment of the best and worst of the world of its day, in order to see clearly where it is to be "in" and where it is to be "not of" that world. And third, the church is called to refuse, a grand refusal to conform to or comply with anything and everything in the world that is against the way of Jesus and his kingdom.

In recent times American Evangelicals, in their foolish failure to learn from the mistakes of Protestant liberalism and their passionate desire to escape any taint from their recent fundamentalist past and to be "relevant" and "seeker sensitive," have largely forgotten the required doubleness or the deliberate ambivalence of this stance. Evangelicals little realize how much they have become the spiritual smiley button of suburban America.

T. S. Eliot was more faithful as well as more realistic when he wrote, "It must be said bluntly that between the Church and the World there is no permanent *modus vivendi* possible."[13] Christopher Dawson used the words of John Henry Newman to make a similar statement: "It is the very function of the Christian to be moving against the world, and to be protesting against the majority of voices."[14] Reinhold Niebuhr was equally blunt: "The modern church regards this mundane interest as its social passion. But it is also the mark of its slavery to society. Whenever religion feels completely at home in the world, it is the salt which has lost its savor. If it sacrifices the strategy of renouncing the world, it has no strategy by which it may convict the world of sin."[15] Earlier, G. K. Chesterton put the issue beyond question when he observed, "A dead thing can go with the stream, but only a living thing can go against it."[16]

Under the power of God, these three factors—committed engagement, cultural discernment and courageous refusal—combine to generate the creative tension with the world that becomes culture shaping. It is still always God's power that changes culture, but it is God's power at work in his people who

are aligned with him, living-in-his-truth and serving his purposes in their generation.

It is true that the greatest power comes when a critical number
of Christians live in truth together in this way in a society. But
even when there is no such critical mass, living-in-truth is the
calling of every individual Christian, for each Christian is
himself or herself the arena in which the struggle takes place
between the pulls and pushes of the world and the call of Jesus.
This means that out of each individual conversion should come
a silent personal revolution that transforms the personal lives of
the converted, which will lead in turn to a social public revolution in wider society, as such a way of life and thought spreads
and is demonstrated by the people of God together.

The Christian, then, does not believe in modern revolutionary
change that is effected from the outside only, for such change is
always too shallow and does not last. But nor is the Christian ever
content with merely being "present" in the world. The key to
changing the world is not simply being there, but an active, transforming engagement of a singularly robust and energetic kind.
And importantly for many Christians today, we must go deeper
than a shallow, purely intellectual understanding of worldviews.
What changes the world is not a fully developed Christian
worldview, but a worldview *actually lived*—in other words, in
Christian lives that are the Word made flesh again.

KEY QUESTION

These principles are easy to say, almost too easy. "In, but not of."
"Not conformed, but transformed." "Yes to their gold, no to their
golden calf." "Against the world, for the world." "No longer, not
yet." The very symmetry of the phrases is mesmerizing, as if
saying so made it so and the beauty and the balance were self-
fulfilling. And surely, we tend to think with the advantage of our

advanced perspective on history, the extremes of the past are so glaringly obvious, which means that we ourselves must be seeing them from a position of perfect balance. So obviously we cannot be mistaken as those earlier generations clearly were.

Really? Nothing perpetuates the imbalances and the extremes more than such a delusion. We are all always more culturally shortsighted than we realize, and doubtless we are more unbalanced too—though in ways that we are not balanced enough to recognize. Think how easily we take for granted our superiority over previous generations. What comes into our minds, for example, when we modern people say "Victorian" or "Puritan"? But that sense of superiority is illusory, a kind of generational illusion, for the simple reason that hindsight enables us to see where those previous generations went wrong, but we cannot see ourselves.

We might be humbler, if not mortified, if we could hear what our grandchildren and their grandchildren will think of us someday—sometimes it is bad enough to know how our children view us now. For doubtless, we are "so twenty-first century," just as the Victorians were children of the nineteenth, and the Puritans of the sixteenth and seventeenth.

Faithful presence is not enough. It is merely the beginning. Jesus was not merely present in the world, but far, far more. He was intensely active: he taught extensively, he healed countless people from all sorts of sickness and disease, he delivered from the domination of evil spirits, he drove out moneychangers from the temple, he raised people from the dead, he confronted hypocrisy, and he set his face toward Jerusalem and his active choice to die. Like him, then, we must be not only present but active, and so dedicated to the world yet so dead to the world to which we are dedicated, that in some small way we too may strike a critical tension with the world that will be the source of the culture-shaping power that only the church can exhibit.

The fact is that the principle is easy to say but hard to follow, for the pressures of the modern world are unrelenting. So if we really wish to be agents of transforming engagement in our time, we have to be constantly asking Lenin's questions: Who? Whom? Is the church shaping the culture, or is the culture shaping the church? But those questions assume other questions that must come even before that. Do we know the world well enough to know how and where it is likely to be squeezing us into its mold? And do we know our faith well enough to know where the mold of our world will be beneficial and where it would be harmful? In sum, we are to be as close as we can be to our Lord's call to us to be in the world but not of it—a challenge that requires not only faithfulness and obedience, but discernment and the willingness to count the cost and say no to the world.

God loves the world—the people of the world, that is—and in this sense so must we. But God does not love the spirit and system of the world that is set over against his kingdom, and neither must we. Thus one positive reason to understand the world is our desire to love the world too and to witness to the world, for the world is the social setting within which people hear what we have to say. Equally, one negative reason to understand the world is the danger of worldliness, for unless we discern its spirit and its shape, the world will always threaten to squeeze us into its mold unawares.

But for our present discussion, the supremely positive reason to understand the world is the dynamic of transforming engagement. When we truly live in the world but are not of it, when we are completely engaged in it though never completely equated with it, we can achieve a critical tension with the world that is born of faithfulness, discernment and refusal. When the church of Jesus lives like that, she becomes—under God—the greatest transforming agency the world has ever seen.

But as ever, *non nobis domine* ("not to us, O Lord"). The glory goes to God and the credit to the shape of the truth of the gospel. It is not we ourselves, but our living-in-truth that changes the world. Our small part is simply to live the truth of the way of Jesus to which we have been called.

A Prayer

O Lord of hosts, God of all power and might above all earthly powers, grant that we may always acknowledge your supreme power and never presume to usurp your place or confuse our tiny insights and our puny power with yours. Grant too that we may so learn to live your truth in every area of our lives that, in some small and imperfect measure, we may be to the world what your Son our Savior Jesus was to the world, and so be true and recognizable followers of his among our fellow people that we may be a credit to his name and a demonstration of his truth. In the name of Jesus, Amen.

Questions for Discussion

1. What is a loyal and distinctive relationship that Christian disciples should have toward the world? Where do you see that lived out well either in history or today?

2. Where are Christians today in danger of usurping God's place by relying on the power of modern insights and technologies rather than the power of God?

3. What does it mean in practice to "live in truth"?

5

THE DYNAMICS OF
THE KINGDOM

Few controversies among Christians are so fruitless as the perennial debate over God's sovereignty and human significance, and it even pokes its nose into the issues we are discussing here too. For when we are thinking of cultural change, is the real work God's or ours, or both? Overall, it is quite clear that the general discussion of the issue has commonly been unproductive. Far too many hours have been wasted, far too much ink has been spilt, and because of the disagreements far too many have dismissed others as not being true Christians and have been dismissed by other Christians in their turn.

Some simple truths are worth recalling in order to apply the point to this discussion. First, the Scriptures show plainly that reality contains both truths, and not just one or the other. God is sovereign, humans are significant, and it was God who made us so. Second, history shows equally plainly that human reason cannot explain both truths. Those who try to do so almost always end up emphasizing one truth to the exclusion of the other, one side majoring on divine sovereignty and the other on human significance. Third, the lesson of the Scriptures and Christian history is that we should rely firmly on both truths, and apply the one we most need when we most need it.

To those who mistrust this approach as simplistic or even underhanded, I would point to numerous examples that show the approach in practice, both in the Scriptures and in the history of the Christian church. The story of St. Paul's shipwreck in the book of Acts is remarkable for many reasons, not least because it is the longest account of such a shipwreck in classical literature. But it is also an unmistakably clear example of holding firmly to both the sovereignty of God and the significance of humans in real life.

On the one hand, the account spells out the sovereignty of God with unmistakable clarity. As the storm worsens and their imminent danger of death comes all too close, an angel sent by God assures Paul, "Do not be afraid, Paul; you must stand before Caesar; and behold, God has granted you all those who are sailing with you." Later, Paul encourages everyone on board to eat some food, "for not a hair from the head of any of you will perish."[1] The two statements are unambiguous and could not be clearer. There is no small print. There are no ifs, buts, qualifications or conditions. God spoke sovereignly, and what God said happened. All 276 of the passengers and crew—some clinging to planks and others to the wreckage of the broken ship—made it to land and were saved. Their ordeal was long and hair-raising, but "they all were brought safely to land."[2]

On the other hand, the account makes equally clear how human significance played a crucial part. Having been assured by God's promise, Paul did not retire to his cabin and sleep through the dangers. Far from it. He was only a prisoner, and he had no status among the fare-paying passengers. But in spite of his subordinate position, he played a leader's part in bringing them all to safety. At one point the sailors tried to escape by themselves, to save their own skins and leave everyone else to drown. It was Paul who prevented them by appealing to the Roman centurion guarding him. "Unless these men remain in the ship, you yourselves cannot be saved."[3]

The logic of Paul's words is worth pondering. Was he qualifying God's original promise that they would all be saved? Was he adding an escape clause, so that God would come out right whatever happened? Wasn't it God who had told him that they would all be rescued, yet here he is introducing a condition. Paul is saying that what the soldiers do in the next few seconds will be decisive for them all. What if the centurion ignored him? Would things have turned out as the angel said, or as Paul said? Why, after all, should a Roman officer follow the advice of a prisoner and a Jew? What if the soldiers tried to obey, but were unable to stop the sailors?

For several agonizing seconds, it must have seemed as if Paul had put the word of the Lord at risk, and it was hanging precariously over the side of the ship like the lifeboat the sailors were launching to save themselves. But the centurion did listen, his soldiers jumped forward to stop the sailors in the nick of time, they all stayed together on board, and eventually they all came safely through. The outcome was just as God had said, but it occurred with Paul's strenuous and highly significant participation playing a key role too.

NO NEED OF GOD?

There is a mystery as to how God's sovereignty and our human significance work together, and there always will be. But what will always remain a mystery is at the same time a reality and not an absurdity. And like the truth of the incarnation and the Trinity, it is an enlightening mystery. It throws light on how we are to live in many areas of our lives, not least in terms of the topic under discussion here: making a difference, transforming society and changing the world. For the mystery sheds light on a simple question that the advanced modern world raises with a vengeance. In a world where we can figure out how to do so much by our own human wisdom and ingenuity, do we really need God to change our world?

In the great temptation in the desert, Jesus firmly reminded the devil of the words of Moses to Israel in Deuteronomy, "Man shall not live on bread alone."[4] But no generation has come closer than ours to being able to do just that—to live self-sufficiently through science alone, through technology alone, through management alone, through medicine alone, or through the many fruits of scholarship and research alone.

So who needs God today? Any "God of the gaps" would find that the modern world has shrunk the gaps almost to the vanishing point. But that would be to express the question with the skepticism of the eighteenth century or the defiance of the recent new atheists. To pose the same question more humbly, and in a manner befitting to faith, do we really need God to change the world or is God expecting us to do it on our own? Where do we draw the line between our trust in God and our reliance on our own God-given wisdom and capabilities? After all, it is God who made us resourceful, and it is God who calls us to be entrepreneurs of life, maximizing our God-given gifts and multiplying the opportunities given us in life.

Ours is unquestionably an extraordinary generation. We can put someone on the moon without God. We can market a car or a perfume without God. We can, it now appears, grow a church without God. We have cracked the codes of our own DNA, and of mystery after mystery. We can devise ways to accomplish tasks earlier generations could only dream of, so do we really need God to transform our societies and change our world? Is God not expecting us to use the best of modern wisdom and get on with it?

Unquestionably, titanic possibilities beckon the world today, and the future lies open to the fearless. In almost every area of human life, our research is laying bare the secrets of how things are and how they can be engineered to fit our human will. This is certainly true in the area we are discussing, for through the best current scholarship we now know more than ever how it is that ideas change the world. Surely then it only remains for us as Christians to use the best of this scholarship (to "plunder the Egyptian gold") and launch a movement to change the world in line with our Christian principles and perspectives. Did we not say that "all truth is God's truth"—so why not modern scholarship too?

Not so fast. The best thinking of today may be excellent, its findings may be true and its applications may be beneficial in a thousand areas. But we must also recognize that there are always two barriers that stand between us and the desired goals of our best ambitions. On the one hand, there is an oddity in the materials we are working on, and an oddity in $\overset{vs}{we}$ who do the work. Because of original sin, the "crooked timber" of our humanity (Immanuel Kant) or the fact that we are "cracked human beings" (John Gray), our best endeavors will always be shot through with ironies and limitations. Many of our grand schemes will not turn out as we hoped and planned. But even when they do, and are not thrown off course by side effects and unintended consequences, our greatest successes will still always be subject to "This too shall pass."

For Christians, the teaching of the Scriptures and history combine to underscore the same lesson in realism and humility. Our best efforts are magnificently worthwhile. We are not condemned to the absurd like Sisyphus as he uselessly rolled the stone up the hill, only for it to roll down again. Under God and after the resurrection of Jesus, our work is never in vain. Our endeavors are worthy and solid, both in themselves and as a down payment on the reality of a far better world that is coming. But in the world as we know it, we cannot live up to Goethe's admonition that we "live resolutely" and "lose the habit of the incomplete."[5] None of our endeavors will meet with unalloyed and lasting success. Few of them will be complete. It is not that our work is ultimately futile or forlorn, as it is for an atheist in a universe without meaning, but incompleteness is written over the best that we can achieve in this life. Truly there is always more to come, and the best is yet to be.

On the other hand, we recognize that, brilliant and bold though our best thinking and actions may be, the kingdom of God is quite simply that—God's kingdom and not ours—so it advances in God's way and not ours. As God reminded his people through the prophet Isaiah,

"For My thoughts are not your thoughts,
Nor are your ways My ways," declares the LORD.
"For *as* the heavens are higher than the earth,
So are My ways higher than your ways
And My thoughts than your thoughts."[6]

The point is not that God's thoughts are unknowable, but that they are different from ours, higher than ours, and therefore they demand that we follow him and not simply our best ideas.

Exactly how God's ways relate to our ways is a mystery that we must not expect to fathom here and now. Here we see through a glass darkly. But it is a mystery that enlightens the partnership to which we have been recruited. God is sovereign and his kingdom advances in his own ways. But we are significant, and while we do not always know the ways that God is using, it is our part in the partnership that we must pursue with energy, humility—and trust.

WISDOM UNDER THE SUN

It is enormously significant that the best modern scholarship throws huge pools of light on our understanding of how ideas influence society and how the world is changed. It is true that all that we can learn this way is knowledge "under the sun," as the preacher in Ecclesiastes puts it, and it is therefore only a matter of the ways of the City of This World. The ways of the City of God will often differ. But the wisdom of the City of Man may be no less accurate for being only "under the sun," and such knowledge can offer practical and helpful insights in countless areas that we ignore at our loss.

What matters is that for Christians, the wisdom of the City of Man never has the last word. The final word always lies with the wisdom of the City of God. We therefore have to clarify a further distinction, not merely between the ways of the City of God and those of the City of Man, but between two different types of lessons from the City of Man. There are *descriptions* of how ideas change the world that are accurate as far as they go, and there are *prescriptions* based on them as to how ideas can or should change the world. The former are often correct and helpful and the latter may be too, but the latter carry greater danger because of the larger role played by values other than Christian values. They therefore require greater assessment. Modern marketing, for example, is usually based on accurate psychological and sociological accounts of how humans behave, though the strategies that follow from them are often highly manipulative and objectionable.

What can we learn from the best current understanding of

how ideas change the world—books such as Randall Collins's *The Sociology of Philosophies* and James Davison Hunter's *To Change the World*? Three foundational lessons have become apparent in recent scholarship. Men and women are each, as Blaise Pascal wrote in his *Pensées,* as fragile as a reed, but they are each a "thinking reed."[7] Thinking is not all-important in human affairs, and disciplines such as the sociology of knowledge have usefully put other factors in place. But human thinking is distinctive and decisive, and it is therefore instructive to learn the lessons of the impact of human thought on human societies from the earliest times down to our own day.

LEADERS OUTWEIGH FOLLOWERS

The first lesson to emerge from recent findings is that the ideas of leaders always outweigh the ideas of followers.[8] Whether leaders are leaders because of their birth, or they are elected or appointed, or whether they gain an informal and charismatic leadership through their character and gifts, leaders are leaders because others follow them. They are the gatekeepers who stand astride the doorways of influence and power and cast a long shadow in their worlds. Not surprisingly, the ideas and opinions of such leaders outweigh the ideas and opinions of those who follow them. Almost by definition, leaders outweigh followers.

Some people argue today that this principle has been rendered obsolete by the new media, which have switched the focus from the few communicating to the many, as in newspapers and television, to the many speaking to the many, as through the Internet. To be sure, we now have powerful voices influencing opinion from people who have never been born to leadership or appointed or elected.

Indeed, today's powerful voice could easily be a teenager operating from a laptop, sitting in his pajamas in his parents' garage in some small town that is considered at the back of beyond. But few butterflies ever really set off earthquakes, and few such people really shift the levers of the world. And when it does happen, it merely underscores the increase of informal and charismatic leadership at the expense of the formal and the established. But generally speaking, it is still leaders who lead and followers who follow.

This point matters for the church, because different Christian traditions have at times gone to different extremes over this issue. Most notably, the Catholic tradition has at times erred on the side of stressing leaders to the point of elitism, and Evangelicals have at times erred equally on the side of populism. The latter of course is still the danger for Evangelicals, for ever since the Second Great Awakening in the nineteenth century, English-speaking Evangelicals have too often been populist to a fault. At times they have been disdainful of education and discipline, suspicious and resentful of leaders and elites, and have tended to put their faith in the opinions of the common person and in the power of mass movements. But this has been at their cost. Like stormy waves breaking on a great rock, their mass movements have at times been impressive, but they have left the rock—and the culture—unmoved.[9]

For many Evangelicals, the contemporary problem has been compounded by a skewed interpretation of Scripture that downplays leadership. "There were not many wise according to the flesh, not many mighty, not many noble," St. Paul wrote of the members of the early church.[10] But somehow the word "many" has been changed to "any," and the very real leaders in the New Testament have been airbrushed away, so that Paul himself, Nicodemus, Manean the boyhood friend of Herod, the governor of Cyprus and many other leaders have been ignored. Saddest of all, this populism has become self-perpetuating at some levels, for the same people who bemoan the hostility of the elites have bred shallow, vulgar and simplistic expressions of faith that few thoughtful people could ever take seriously—and which have little chance of changing anything, let alone the world.

THE CENTER OUTWEIGHS THE PERIPHERY

The second lesson to grow clearer is that ideas are more powerful when they are exerted at the center of a society, rather than the periphery. Many countries have cities that exercise a disproportionate influence on the whole country. Often these cities are the capital city, and occasionally the capital is geographically and culturally central. In France, for example, all roads lead to Paris.

In other countries, such as the United States, there is no single cultural center. Instead, there are several. Washington, DC, is the political center; New York, the economic center; and Los Angeles, the media and entertainment center. Wherever the geographical center is in the US—it is actually in Kansas—I have never yet met an American who knows exactly where it is, and the reason is obvious. The geographical center is culturally irrelevant, whereas the cultural centers are all-powerful. For, as sociologists Randall Collins and James Hunter have demonstrated beyond argument, it is the centers of cultural power in any society that define reality, set the agendas and create the fashions.

Once again, other religious believers, such as Jews, and other Christian traditions, such as Catholicism, have had a far shrewder appreciation of this point than most Evangelicals. Jews and Catholics have tended naturally to plant their flags at the centers of power—for example, the strength of the Jews in New York or of Catholic institutions such as Georgetown University and Georgetown Hospital in Washington, DC. Evangelicals, in contrast, have lived true to their populist leanings, and all too often have taken to the backwaters and the out-of-the-way places—resulting in their weakened influence on culture.

NETWORKS OUTWEIGH INDIVIDUALS
AND INSTITUTIONS

The third lesson we must take into account is that ideas spread best through networks, rather than through either individuals or institutions. Christians of all traditions have a far better record here, and the roll call of influential Christian networks is illustrious—the twelve apostles, the Benedictines and the many influential Catholic orders they spawned, the White Horse Inn in Cambridge, the Moravians and their hundred-year prayer meeting, the cell groups of John Wesley, the Clapham Circle of William Wilberforce, the Inklings discussing their ideas at Oxford's tiny pub The Eagle and Child, and so on.

The potential of new forms of such networks in the age of the new social media is unimaginable, and it will undoubtedly play a leading part in the spread of Christian ideas in the global era. In sum, all three of these lessons have immense significance for understanding the growth of the Church in the past and the advance of the kingdom of God in the future. We must therefore ponder them, and learn from them all that we can.

Yet for all their accuracy and practical benefits, these lessons are the still wisdom "under the sun." As products of the City of This World, they would not only apply to Jesus but to the ideas of Confucius, Gautama Buddha, Muhammad, Mahatma Gandhi and Richard Dawkins too. We therefore have to go further and look at the ways of the City of God, and how they may differ—for differ they will because the City of God is an entirely different order.

Many Christian writers who stress the three points above rarely go on to do justice to the dynamics of the kingdom. Their understanding is true as far as it goes, but it never rises to be more than insights "under the sun." Yet as Christopher Dawson pointed out, we should not be surprised that the kingdom has its own distinctive ways. "We have no right to expect that Christian principles will work in practice in the simple way that a political system may work. The Christian order is a supernatural order. It has its own principles and its own laws which are not those of the visible world and which may often seem to contradict them. Its victories may be found in apparent defeat and its defeats in material success."[11] In the end it must always be the City of God that is decisive for us. God's ways are different from our ways, and God's work must always be done in God's way.

THE SPIRIT OF GOD LEADS

How do the ways of the City of God differ from the ways of the City of Man? And how do we live by the dynamics of the City of God while still respecting the lessons from the City of Man? How do we follow the example of St. Paul, who followed the prompting of the Holy Spirit while still always aiming to bring the gospel to Rome at the heart of the Roman Empire? There is no single answer to this question, and Christians will differ honorably in answering it. And as I mentioned earlier, we also have to distinguish between the descriptions and the prescriptions of the City of Man. There is no such thing as a value-free description, so even descriptions have to be examined with care, but there is no question about the greater difference between descriptions and prescriptions.

My own view of the ways of the City of God has been shaped by my reading of the Scriptures and Christian history, though with the Scriptures given the supreme authority. The first thing that is surely beyond doubt in such a perspective is that in the kingdom of God, God himself leads, and he leads his church and his people through his Spirit.

This fact is unmistakable in the book of Acts, which as often pointed out could easily be called the Acts of the Holy Spirit rather than the Apostles. Jesus called the twelve disciples to follow him, then the seventy and then the wider movement of his followers. After his death and resurrection, he commanded them to wait in Jerusalem for the promised gift of his Spirit who would be to them what he was in person during his life on earth. And once the Spirit of God had come down to them at Pentecost, it was the Spirit, and not Peter, James, John and Paul, who was the true leader of the fledgling church and led to its rapid and astonishing expansion.

How did the gospel come to Africa? (And it is striking that it reached Africa before it came to Europe.) The Spirit spoke to Philip and sent him to the road where he met the officer from Ethiopia, who was converted and took the gospel to the heart of Africa.

How did the gospel come to Europe? Clearly, Greece was not in Paul's "next steps." He was determined to continue his journey to Asia Minor and Bithynia, but he found himself blocked, checked and frustrated, and it was only then that he became open to the vision of the man from Macedonia and the famous cry to "come over and help us!" As one historian described the result, when that unknown rabbi crossed unheralded from Troas to Philippi at the orders of the Spirit of God, it made more impact on world history than even the great sea battle of Actium a few miles away, the battle that settled the fate of the Roman Empire after the assassination of Julius Caesar.

How did the gospel get to the Gentiles, who include the great majority of us and most Christians through the ages and across the world? It was the Spirit of God who blew apart the die-hard prejudices of the apostle Peter, and sent him from Joppa to Caesarea to share the good news of Jesus with those long considered "dogs" and "unclean" outsiders.

And how did the missionary movement—the single most significant Christian initiative after Jesus and the gift of the Holy Spirit—start in the first place? No local committee, church-wide council or international congress was behind it. There was no headhunter or executive search involved. Rather, "the Holy Spirit said, 'Set apart for Me Barnabas and Saul for the work to which I have called them.'"[12] And soon the world was "turned upside down," and was never the same again.[13]

This first point—that it should be the Spirit who leads—embarrasses many of us and our traditions today. On the one hand, the Holy Spirit is the neglected, if not forgotten, member of the Trinity for many in the Western church today. For some, the cause is the bureaucratic institutionalizing of the medieval church and the emphasis on saints and mediators rather than God himself. For others, the reason goes back to a post-Reformation dryness that stressed the Word of God at the expense of the Spirit of God. For still others, the root lies in a general inclination to see the world with the lenses of Enlightenment naturalism, and so to suffer from its tone deafness and reality blindness to the spiritual realm. Yet for others, the Spirit of God is neglected because of the weird, wild and wonderful things done in his name.

Further, our typical modern mentality leaves us with no inclination to look or to listen to the Spirit of God anyway. Surely, we almost say, we have no need to. Never have we been better able to figure it out and do it all ourselves. Just give us a yellow pad or a white board, and within minutes we can chart the best course to adopt. Vision, Mission, Objectives, Personnel, Budget, Next Steps, Timeline, Measurable Outcomes, Best Practices—the headings flow naturally, and the thinking can be applied to any project.

Who needs God today any more than we need the great consulting companies? For we are all management experts now. We know the best way to market a product or plan an event. We have all the polling statistics we need at our fingertips. We have a consultant, an expert or a specialist on hand for anything and everything. To be sure, we may pray briefly "fore and aft" as we proceed. But this is the age of do-it-yourself, and there is no one and nothing else that we really need, thank you.

Need it be said that in thinking ourselves so competent, we set ourselves up to become clueless, and thinking that we are so smart, we turn out to become a laughingstock. There is always a gap between human motives and intentions and historical outcomes, for the idea that all we intend will happen, and that all that will happen is what we intended, is the heart of the planners' fallacy. As T. S. Eliot reminded his generation, culture can never be planned. "Culture can never be wholly conscious—there is always more to it than we are conscious of; and it cannot be planned because it is also the unconscious background of all our planning."[14]

More importantly, all our modern savvy may be wonderful beyond words, but compared with the strategic leadership of the Spirit of God, it is puny to the point of absurdity. Only a fool could mistake a bauble for crown, and only a simpleton could confuse the information and knowledge of the City of Man for the real wisdom of the City of God. Even in the grand age of leadership seminars, management studies and project management, and the countless bestsellers on the umpteen secrets of business success, it is the Spirit of God who leads the advance of the kingdom of God.

SURPRISING REVERSALS

The second common feature of the way of the kingdom of God is its surprising reversals. To trust in God is to let God be God, and to undercut all grounds for human boasting by giving him the praise and credit that is due to him alone. For a start, as we have seen, God's ways are not our ways, and his wisdom is so far above ours as to be a mystery beyond our ken. Add to that the fact that God opposes the proud, and all who rear their heads in pride to vaunt their self-sufficiency or their arrogance before him.

But how does God counter such human pride? On the one hand, he does so through the most brilliant and surprising subversion ever conceived, and once again it is not by might, nor by power, and at first it is not even by God's Spirit. It is by his Son. So, wonder of all mouth-stopping wonders, what the shepherds saw when they abandoned their sheep and hurried down to Bethlehem was the one they worshiped as God Almighty lying defenseless in a crib, who one day would die deserted and derelict on a cross. Just so did supreme power mask itself as weakness, unbounded wealth take on the guise of poverty, unfathomable wisdom arrive incognito as foolishness, and ultimate worth come down looking humble to the point of being contemptible.

But that is not the end of God's great smack in the eye for human pride. For God chooses messengers who are every bit as surprising as he himself. Who else would have chosen as a special servant the tongue-tied Moses; the slip-of-a-lad Samuel; the unlikely, youngest-brother-of-eight David; the shy, hypersensitive introvert Jeremiah; the unmarried Mary; or the rough, desert-living John the Baptist? But as Mary recognized in her heartfelt song of praise, reversals were God's signature way of operating, and the hallmark of his kingdom.

> He has done mighty deeds with His arm;
> He has scattered *those who were* proud in the thoughts of
>   their heart.

He has brought down rulers from *their* thrones,
And has exalted those who were humble.
HE HAS FILLED THE HUNGRY WITH GOOD THINGS;
And sent away the rich empty-handed.[15]

Mary's son and John's cousin continued in the same subversive way as he was born. As he announced the good news of
the kingdom, he took delight in all its surprising reversals.
Blessed are the poor in spirit. The first would be last, and the last
first. The humble would be exalted, and the exalted humbled.
Whoever wished to save their lives would lose them, whereas
those prepared to lose their lives for his sake would find them.
Those who wanted the best seats in the kingdom would have to
be the servants of everyone else. The one who is least is the one
who is great. The wisdom of God had been revealed to infants,
and not to the wise and the intelligent. Tax collectors and pros-
titutes will enter the kingdom before the scribes and the Phar-
isees. The stone that the builders rejected has turned out to be
the chief cornerstone. And so it goes.

And so it still goes today as it has done down the centuries.
Nietzsche called for a "revaluation of all values," but what he
announced he was impotent to effect. Jesus said it and did it. He
initiated the grandest reversal of all time. The kingdom of God
is an upside-down, back-to-front, inside-out kingdom that stuns
our expectations and blasts us out of our ruts and our prejudices.
Above all, it rebukes our pride and pricks the bubbles of our
pretensions. God is different from us, he works differently from
us, and it is up to us to mirror his will and his ways. The City of
God is not the City of This World. God's work is to be done in
God's way. It shines far clearer in St. Francis, the jongleur of the
poor from Assisi, than in Pope Julius, the gold-armored head of
Christendom who actually led his soldiers in battle and commis-

sioned some of history's finest artists to glorify his residence and celebrate his reign.

So yes, we strive for excellence. We know that nothing less than our best is worthy of our Lord. Our concern is always to achieve our utmost for his highest. We know that leaders have more influence than followers, that the center of a culture has an influence that far outweighs the periphery, that kings outweigh commoners, that the rich can get far more done than the poor, and that the well-educated know far more than the average person.

We know all that, we respect all that, and we take it seriously—and yet, and yet. So we are also always ready for the surprising voice, the far-from-obvious leader, the last-person-you-would-ever-think would be the key player. And yes, we are always ready to recognize God's nobodies and God's fools. For these may be the truly anointed ones prepared to be seen and treated as nobodies and fools for Christ's sake, whom God uses far more than we who are the obvious ones for God to use.

GREAT CULTURE A BY-PRODUCT

The third common feature of the way of the kingdom of God is that distinctive culture is more often a by-product than a goal. As John Baillie observed of civilization, "There is a sense, then, in which the ages to whom we owe our Christian civilization valued that civilization less highly than we do today. They valued it indeed, but gave it only a secondary place. It may be said to have come into being as a by-product of something immeasurably more to be treasured."[16]

What did Baillie mean? As people of faith, we are each to follow our calling to the maximum of our abilities and to the full extent of our lives, living to the glory of God and with an eye to our neighbors' needs. It is not up to us to save and to manage the world, especially in the global era, for trying to do so will end up either in windy abstractions or in the paralysis that comes from being overwhelmed. Only God can handle the whole world. The world is not ours to manage or to save. Our task is to focus on our individual callings in engaging with the world, to trust that others are following theirs too, and to leave to God the masterminding of the grand outcome. That call to each Christian to pursue their individual calling in engaging with the world is what lies behind the maxim mentioned earlier, "Let a thousand flowers bloom!"

T. S. Eliot underscored the same point heavily. One definite conclusion from thinking about culture and civilization is that

> Culture is the one thing that we cannot deliberately aim at. It is the product of a variety of more or less harmonious activities, each pursued for its own sake: the artist must concentrate upon his canvas, the poet upon his typewriter, the civil servant upon the just settlement of particular problems as they present themselves upon his desk, each according to the situation in which he finds himself. Even if these conditions with which I am concerned, seem to the reader to represent desirable social aims, he must not leap to the conclusion that these aims can be fulfilled solely by deliberate organisation.[17]

This point sits oddly with us today, for we live in an age when we take great pride in our purposes, our plans and our projects. Everything has to be "purpose filled," "intentional" and "by design." For most people, their achievements may fall short of their ambitions, but the illusion is still common that, like Friedrich Nietzsche, we can write the story of our lives according to the grand theme, "Thus I willed it." Add to this mindset the capacities empowered by modern management, and the dream is inspired of how we can change the world through our own endeavors. And today the final touch is the fashionable discussion of how we must each think through the "legacy" that we wish to leave behind us when we die.

Over all this grand humanistic conceit the words should be written, "As if they knew." For all such talk assumes that we know completely who we are, that we know completely how we need to do what we wish to do, and that we know completely what we have done, which we then wish to leave as our legacy for our children and the next generation.

But we quite simply do not know. We do not fully know ourselves. We do not fully know how to do what we want to do. And we certainly do not fully know what is the legacy that we are leaving behind. We do not understand history and we certainly do not control history. Only God knows the answer to all these issues, so our human knowledge will always be incomplete— even with the most successful.

William Wilberforce is an inspiring model for many, but he was unusual. As is well known, he wrote in his journal at the age of twenty-eight that God had set before him two great objectives—the suppression of the slave trade and the reformation of manners, or moral standards. He then spent the next forty-seven years of his life pursuing these momentous goals, and achieved the first objective last, just three days before his death in 1833. But inspiring though his heroic example is, we need to remember that it is also highly uncommon. As one admirer said, it is extremely rare in most lives for the "termination of a person's labors" and the "termination of their lives" to be crowned with such success and with such symmetry.

Most of our lives are closer to the heroes of Hebrews 11. By faith these men and women rose to trust God and follow the visions God had given them with courage and perseverance, but they also died in faith without seeing the fulfillment of the promises and the fruition of the visions. At best they hailed them from afar in faith. But that was enough to make them strangers and exiles in the world of their times, and that was enough too for God to declare that he was not ashamed to be their God and to prepare a city for them. In other words, even the best and highest of our human endeavors usually have a single word written over them—incomplete. As Reinhold Niebuhr wrote well,

> Nothing that is worth doing can be achieved in our lifetime; therefore we must be saved by hope. Nothing which is true or beautiful or good makes complete sense in any immediate context of history; therefore we must be saved by faith. Nothing we do, however virtuous, can be accomplished alone; therefore we are saved by love. No virtuous act is quite as virtuous from the standpoint of our friend or foe as it is from our standpoint. Therefore we must be saved from the final form of love which is forgiveness.[18]

But ignorance and incompleteness are not the only reason why great culture is usually a by-product rather than a goal. The more positive reason is that the kingdom of God is organic rather than organizational. Sowers sow. Seeds grow naturally, automatically and invisibly. From such seeds, a great tree grows, in which birds can nest—or a great yield ripens, with wheat and tares growing together until separated at the harvest, or yet again, the yeast inserted in the dough acts and spreads until the bread rises as a delicious and nourishing loaf.

As T. S. Eliot insisted: "Culture is something that must grow; you cannot build a tree, you can only plant it, and care for it, and wait for it to mature in its due time; and when it is grown you must not complain if you find that from an acorn has come an oak and not an elm-tree."[19] And so it is with the kingdom, as the seeds of faith ripen in countless lives into the fruit of the Spirit, and the people of God grow, ripen and bear more fruit in ways that defy all expectations.

Once again, the mindset of the kingdom of God and the mentalities bred by modern management and marketing are often incompatible. God's ways are not our ways, and our ways are not God's ways. We can plunder the Egyptian gold, but woe betide the church that uses it to worship a golden calf. Citizens of the City of God still reside in the City of This World, and their lives will intersect at a thousand points. But for us, whenever a clash occurs, it is the ways of the City of God that must prevail.

Put differently again, Jesus tells his followers to seek first God's kingdom, "and all these things will be added to you." We are to trust and obey God, and to follow his call in every inch of our lives, in every second of our time, and with every gift with which we have been endowed. And we are then to leave the result as well as the assessment to God.

Just so did the unknown men and women of the Middle Ages build the great cathedrals and the first universities. Just so did Dante Alighieri write his poetry, Johann Sebastian Bach compose his music, Rembrandt paint his paintings, Dostoevsky pen his novels, and Gerard Manley Hopkins, Emily Dickinson, Christina Rossetti and T. S. Eliot write their poetry nearer our own time. We glory in all the beauty, truth and goodness brought into the world, as well as the peace, justice, freedom and human dignity, but such great culture is usually a by-product and not a conscious objective. The kingdom of God is our goal, in all its fully orbed richness throughout our daily lives. All the rest is the added value that, by God's grace, comes with it.

It is a peculiar modern superstition that to achieve success in any area we have to make that area the be all and end all of our lives—and live and breathe for that alone. (Vince Lombardi: "Winning isn't everything, it's the only thing.") Down that way lies the path to idolatry, obsession, restlessness, cut-throat rivalry, and a life marked by either arrogance or bitter regrets. If our best strivings are to remain truly human, they need a goal and a standard outside us to challenge us always to aim higher, but also to bring in fresh air and keep life in perspective. Our goals, tasks and missions are never themselves God. If we try to make them so, they will be idols. Only God is God, and therefore such a goal and standard above all our endeavors. Again, we are to "seek first His kingdom . . . and all these things will be added to you."[20]

Our task, then, is clear, though challenging. We must critique the "Christian West" and any other expressions of Christian culture, but we must never abandon the proper link between Christian faithfulness and culture making. Whether our prospects as Christians today look bright or dismal, whether the tide of modern culture is flowing our way or against us, whether we are strong in numbers or almost seem to be on our own, such external factors are all irrelevant. We must each follow our calling, pursue our utmost for his highest in every possible way and count unquestioningly on the dynamics of the kingdom of God, and then, knowing our own chronic ignorance and the probable incompleteness of our endeavors, trust the outcome to God.

Such are the sure and certain dynamics of the kingdom that God's work done in God's way will never lack for God's blessing and God's fruitfulness—and in ways that are far beyond our best planning and our wildest imaginings.

A Prayer

Lord Jesus Christ, our Savior, Redeemer, Master and Friend, we give thanks for your divine love that sought for us when we went astray, brought us back when we were lost, and humbled itself to be seen as weak, poor and foolish in order to subvert our pride, our ignorance and our stupidity. Grant that we may ever strive to serve you with the excellence you deserve, while always attuned to how your ways are not our ways, so that we may embody the unlikely surprises and the uniqueness of your astonishing kingdom. In the name of Jesus, Amen.

Questions for Discussion

1. Which of the three insights of today's superb scholarship are we most in need of in the West today?

2. How close are churches you know to following the three kingdom principles?

3. How do we relate the world's best insights with the principles of the kingdom?

Our Golden Age Is Ahead

O ne of the newer Oxford colleges is Linacre College, founded in 1962 and named after Thomas Linacre. He is hardly known today, but in his time in the sixteenth century, he was the preeminent Renaissance scholar in England, court physician to King Henry VIII, founder of the Royal College of Physicians, and the honored teacher and friend of both Erasmus and Sir Thomas More.

As a scholar and fellow of All Souls College, Oxford, Linacre was well versed in both Greek and Latin, but he lived before the Reformation, when the Bible was restricted to the clergy. So he had never read it in depth. One day a friend who was a priest gave him a copy of the four Gospels, Matthew, Mark, Luke and John, and he studied them in full and in the original language for the first time. Linacre thought for a while, and then handed them back to the priest with the remark, "Either these are not the Gospels, or we are not Christians!"

Not long afterward, Linacre's brilliant student Erasmus made the same point in his scathing and subversive indictment of

Christian corruption, *In Praise of Folly*. And it was not much longer before, in 1517, a young Augustinian monk hammered ninety-five theses to the door of the Castle Church in Wittenberg to protest the same gap between Christ and his church, and the protest movement that became the Reformation began.

The Reformation was simultaneously the Western church's greatest necessity and its greatest tragedy, for in its brilliant but terrible light we can see with an unmistakable clarity the three major besetting sins of the church's long engagement with culture—secularization, corruption and division.

Secularization happens whenever the church is so "in" the world that she is "of the world" and unrelievedly worldly—when she is engaged but equated, and without remainder, so much so that she is indistinguishable from her day and age (the original meaning of *saeculum*). Such secularization from the inside is far more deadly to the church than attacks from the outside. It has happened many times in the church's history in larger and smaller ways, both before the Reformation and afterward, but who can deny that the Renaissance popes and cardinals were little more than secular princelings? They claimed to walk in the shoes of the Fisherman and to sit in St. Peter's chair, but there was little of Jesus or the way of Jesus evident in their personal lives or in their conduct of public affairs.

Erasmus witnessed the return of Pope Julius II in his golden armor after his victory at the Battle of Bologna, and wondered aloud whether he was really the disciple of Jesus or in fact the heir of his great namesake Julius Caesar. Not for nothing was Julius known as *il papa terribile* ("the terrifying pope"). When his successor, Giovanni de' Medici, was elected Pope Leo X, he remarked famously, "Since God has given us the papacy, let us enjoy it." And there is no doubt that he did, as the chroniclers of his time record in lurid detail. Later, Pope Urban VIII, sponsor of the legendary sculptor and architect Gian Lorenzo Bernini and creator of much of the more recent glory of Rome, was so unbridled in his personal vanity and ambition as pope that it was said of him: *L'église, c'est moi!* ("The church is me!")

Corruption happens whenever the church, which has become that worldly, so relies on the powers of the world that she grows powerful and is corrupted by that power. Who can doubt that the Borgia popes were more reliant on the power of the sword and the money of the bankers than the power of the gospel? The famous maxim, "Power tends to corrupt, and absolute power corrupts absolutely," came from the pen of Lord Acton, a devout but freedom-loving Catholic.[1] And even earlier than the Borgias, Bernard of Clairvaux had protested against the corruptions of the twelfth-century Curia, "Is not all Italy a yawning gulf of insatiable avarice and rapacity for the spoil it offers?"[2] The church, he wrote, "is full of ambitious men; the time has gone for being shocked at the enterprising efforts of ambition; we think no more of it than a robber's cave thinks of the spoils of the wayfarers."[3]

And division happens when those who protest against such unfaithfulness are forced to leave the church out of faithfulness, or are simply forced out. There is no doubt that Catholicism has demonstrated an astonishing capacity to absorb and domesticate dissent of all kinds and remain itself, far more so than Protestantism. But the toxic worldliness and corruption of the pre-Reformation Church of Rome required an institutional strength and elasticity that not even the Catholic Church could muster to save itself. There must be no romantic airbrushing of that chapter of Christian history.

Yet who can quarrel with the fact that the divisions of Christendom and their consequences are one of the major factors leading to the centuries-long rejection of the church in the West? On the one hand, the divisions of the church are a direct disobedience to the desire and the prayer of our Lord in the Garden of Gethsemane. In addition, the divisions and the warring they produced are the central reason why the Christian faith is now seen as socially divisive and disruptive rather than constructive and uniting. The divided church is a disobedient church. There are always issues, such as truth and orthodoxy, which must be fought for, but "fought for" in a decisively Christlike way. When Christians fight with fellow Christians, there is an important sense in which they have both already failed.

In sum, the Reformation was desperately necessary, but the Reformation was also tragic, and it exposed the church to the gaze and scrutiny of the world as a church that was secularized, corrupt and divided. It was a tragic necessity that was caused by dire evil—like the division of Israel after the reign of King Solomon, about which the prophet said on behalf of the Lord, "This thing has come from Me."[4]

Those who rightly lament the division, usually Roman Catholics, must also give a full and candid account of the cause. For it was the Catholic Church that in the interests of its temporal power most denied the gospel in its abuse of truth, justice and freedom. Looked at from the perspective of the last millennium, this division is the main reason for the rejection of the Christian faith from its central position and role in the Western world. As Christopher Dawson argues, as a Catholic himself, it was the corruptions and divisions of Christendom that led to the secularization of Europe. "The convinced secularists were an infinitesimal minority of the European population, but they had no need to be strong since the Christians did their work for them."[5] It was also shocking but revealing that even before the fall of Constantinople in 1453, the Byzantine Christians preferred to be under Islam rather than the papacy. Their telltale slogan said it all, "Better the prophet's turban than the pope's tiara."

Sadly the story of this tragedy is not over, and there have been many times in the history of the church when the same protest has been necessary. Confronting the smug orthodoxy of the Protestant church in nineteenth-century Denmark, Kierkegaard leveled the same charge as Linacre in his passionate *Attack upon Christendom*: "The Christianity of the New Testament simply does not exist," and again: "'Christendom' is . . . the betrayal of Christianity."[6] Does not the same protest need to be made all over again today? For the gap between the gospel and the church has grown again in many of our traditions, and much of the Protestant church in the Western world is as decisively in need of reformation as the Catholic Church was before the Reformation. It is true that much of the Catholic Church has proved more resistant to the seductions of modernity than Protestantism, but mainly because, with modernity, "to be further behind is to be better off."

Woodrow Wilson, a self-professed progressive in politics, once described the best leaders as people who were so in tune with the opinion of their generation that they could walk in front of the crowd and show others the path they should take—to which came an apt reply, "This is nothing but the despicable principle of that great demagogue, Ledru-Rollin: 'I am their leader, so I have to follow them.'"[7]

Protestant liberalism in its extremes, such as the writings of John Shelby Spong, significant parts of Evangelicalism, and now even some progressive Catholics have shown themselves so caught up in the passing spirit of the age that they act not so much as leaders of the crowd as streetwalkers eager for some new trade with the latest idea on the streets. Kierkegaard famously called such people "kissing Judases"—Christians who betray Jesus with an interpretation. But whether mild or extreme, too much of the English-speaking world seems bent on fulfilling T. S. Eliot's comment that "the Anglo-Saxons display a capacity for *diluting* their religion, probably in excess of that of any other race."[8]

It has often been observed that the Jacobinism of the French Revolution and the Bolshevism of the Russian would both have been unthinkable without the role of priests, ex-priests, seminaries and religious schools. Along with the numerous philosophizing clerics who advocated revolution, both Voltaire and Diderot received a Jesuit education, and the former owed his deism to an abbé; Jean-Jacques Rousseau put his philosophy into the mouth of a vicar; Josef Stalin and Anastas Mikoyan were seminarians; and it was a French pastor, Claude Royer, who was a member of the Jacobin Club in Paris and called for the launch of the reign of terror ("Let us make terror the order of the day!")[9]

It would be idle to speculate what terrible new order today's trendy clerics and faithless Christian activists are greasing the shipway for. But we need not wait for the outcome. The truth is that the greatest enemy of the Western church is not the state or any ideology such as atheism, but the world and the spirit of the age. Anything less than a full-blooded expression of the Christian faith has no chance of standing firm against the assaults and seductions of the advanced modern world. So when the church becomes worldly, she betrays her Lord, and she also fails to live up to her calling to be dangerously different and thus to provide deliverance from the world by a power that is not of the world. When "saving us from ourselves" has become the widespread problem of the advanced modern world, the worldly church has no supernatural salvation to offer and stands in shame as desperately needing saving herself.

But that is not the end of it. The worldly church is not only corrupt but cowardly, for much contemporary worldliness is a *voluntary capitulation* to the spirit and system of the age. There are times when the powers of the age openly seek to seduce the church or brutally subjugate her to their own purposes. That can be bad enough, as witnessed by the widespread compromise of Russian Orthodoxy under Stalinism or Lutheranism under Hitler. But the contemporary worldliness of parts of the Western church, as exemplified differently by the extremes of either the Episcopal Church in America or the emergent Evangelicals, is in one sense worse. As Jesus said, "You will know them by their fruit." Just wait long enough for their ideas to ripen, and in case after case it turns out that the much-trumpeted "new kind of Christianity for a new world" turns out to be the old kind of compromise and heresy. Such worldliness is inexcusable because it is self-chosen, naively and breathlessly self-chosen, and in many cases foolish beyond all comprehension.

Carl F. H. Henry, the great Evangelical theologian and leader used to say of his fellow believers in the United States, "Earlier, it was next to impossible to get Evangelicals out into the culture. Now it is equally impossible to get the culture out of Evangelicals." In its shallow and noisy worldliness, much Evangelicalism has become little more than the culture-religion of the declining Christian consensus that once dominated America.

Semper reformanda, the Reformation principle of the need for constant, ongoing reformation is as vital as ever. But the question we should ask ourselves is not "Am I Reformed?" but "Am I being reformed, and am I reforming?" Many of us look at ourselves, and we look around at much of the church in the West today, with the vast mismatch between its still-large numbers and its increasing lack of integrity and influence, and we can only say with tears and a heavy heart, "Either there is something wrong with the way of Jesus, or there must be something wrong with us."

And of course, to our shame we surely know the answer all too well.

ONLY ONE CHRISTIAN

Marcus Tullius Cicero, the great Roman statesman, philosopher and orator, wrote that, "Not to know what happened before you were born, that is to be always a boy, to be forever a child." We have too many "forever children" in the Western church today, Christians with no appreciation of the past, who are condemned to live Peter Pan lives in a never-never land of the present, with little knowledge of the past (or much care for the future) to inspire their heroism, to season their wisdom and to protect their steps from the pitfalls into which previous generations have fallen.

One might think that two thousand years after Jesus, we would be the wisest generation of Christians who ever lived. Surely it is our privilege to be inspired by the past, and rendered almost error-proof through the rich course of lessons provided for us by those who have gone before us—and fallen before us, whether into heresies or scandals.

Sadly that is not the case. Those most aware of history are also those most humbled by the certainty that we may make all the same mistakes again, and our own original ones too. A young American lady once told Theodor Mommsen that America's mistakes should be excused because America was only a young nation. "Madame," the eminent historian replied, "your nation has had open before it the whole history of Europe from the beginning; and without exception you have consistently copied every mistake Europe has ever made."[10]

Woe betide the foolish whose power is so powerful and whose success is so successful that they presume they can afford not to learn. It is our privilege to have at our disposal the lessons of two thousand years of the church's engagement with culture. The chief lesson of the last two thousand years is that there is no one Christian culture and there is no perfect Christian culture,

so there is no golden age behind us. Our golden age lies ahead—
when, and only when, our Lord returns.

Doubtless this elementary lesson should have been clear from
the very start. After all, we Christians are those who take original
sin seriously, our own included. And as Nietzsche rightly said,
there has only ever been one real Christian and he was crucified
on the cross. All the rest of us as followers of Christ throughout
history, even the great saints, have always been less than consistently and completely Christian. While we are in this life and on
this earth we never get beyond the "not yet."

Indeed, it has always been a mark of the greatest saints that
the nearer others thought they were to God, the more they were
aware of their sins and shortcomings. When Robert Murray
M'Cheyne, the brilliant young Scottish preacher from St. Peter's
Dundee, was once congratulated for his saintliness, he replied
sharply: "Madame, if you could see into my heart, you would
spit in my face."

That same humility must be brought to our understanding of
Christian culture, and this should have been understood in principle from the start. Wherever God has not given us clear and
authoritative instructions as to how we are to conduct our lives,
we are free to pursue our own solutions within the guidelines of
the principles God has given us. But that means that our best
solutions will always be *a* Christian way of doing things, and a
less than perfectly Christian way of doing things. They are not
the Christian way.

In the light of God's principles, we can say that certain ways
of doing things that contradict those principles are *not* Christian,
but we can never say that *one way alone is.* In that sense, there
is no one "Christian economics" any more than there is one
"Christian retirement plan," one "Christian political party," or
one Christian anything.

To believe otherwise, and then to claim that our best ways of doing things are "the Christian way," is the fallacy of particularism. Again, there are ways of doing things that we can say with certainty are *not* Christian, but in most areas there is no *one particular way* that we should say alone is Christian. Identifying any particular form of doing things as "Christian" plain and simple is a dangerous mistake. It confuses the absolute with the relative, and the permanent with the passing, and so paves the way for the rejection of the faith along with the passing form, whatever it happens to be.

This caution applies equally to our attitudes to cultures. Doubtless all Christians have their favorite periods of Christian history, which to them represent the golden age of faith. The Orthodox prize the age of the early Fathers. Catholics talk reverently of the medieval world and "the great age of faith." Protestants elevate the Reformation and its "recovery of the gospel and the Scriptures." Evangelicals take great pride and courage from the First Great Awakening and its potent combination of the preaching of the gospel and the spawning of myriad social reforms. And Pentecostals and charismatics hark back to the Azusa Street revival and its triggering of one of the greatest and still continuing missionary advances in the history of the Christian church.

Yet all these periods were at best more or less Christian, and today their flaws, their blind spots, their unintended consequences could be enumerated along with their undisputed blessings. This is not to argue for moral equivalence, to confuse truth with power and plausibility, to minimize the importance of different Christian traditions, or to make the mistake of thinking that theological criteria do not matter.

Truth always matters supremely. God is a God of truth. He is the true One, he acts truly, he speaks truly, and his truth must always be our supreme criterion and concern.

Indeed, to be disloyal to God's truth, as the extremes of Protestant liberalism have been for two hundred years and are flagrantly so today, is a failure of love as well as intellect. Unfaithfulness is a matter of adultery and not merely apostasy. Without such a commitment to truth, there can be no reformation, and no possibility of reformation, for truth is the standard by which the need for reformation is judged and the standard by which any reformation proceeds. Without such truth, there could be no difference between reformation and deformation. Without such truthfulness, the world would be all gray and everything would be reduced to "Says who?"

But that said, it is also true that all Christian cultures are flawed, just as all of us as Christians are fallen. Only when we meet God face to face will we have become what he is making us to be, and only when God establishes his kingdom fully will we have a culture that is truly, completely and absolutely worthy of the name Christian. In short, the golden age for the Christian always lies ahead, and until that day our highest endeavors must always be regarded with realism and a wry humility. Before we knew God we fell short of God's standards, and it was grace that rescued us and drew us to faith. But now that we know God we still fall short of God's standards, and it is still grace that we need to rescue us and make us more what we should be. Once again, "not yet" and "incomplete" are written over even our best ideas and endeavors. We thank God for the different traditions and for the best of the great ages of faith that lie behind us, but our golden age lies ahead when the Messiah returns.

THE GOD OF SURPRISES
Along with this grand foundational lesson, there are three other lessons from history that can challenge and hearten us today, because each of them reminds us that God is a God of

surprises, and it is always God who has the last word.

History's first paradoxical lesson is that *times of the greatest success often carry the seeds of the greatest failure*. It is a sad but highly significant fact that the greatest evils that the Christian church perpetrated on the world came out of what was considered the most consistent and completely Christian society, not only of its own time but in the entire world up until then—Christendom.

The setting of St. Augustine's *City of God* was actually quite remarkable in a way that many people miss. For the Bishop of Hippo was not only answering the pagans who blamed the Christians for the fall of Rome, but he was challenging the Christians of his day to distinguish their citizenship in the City of God from their citizenship in the City of Man—Rome. Since their true citizenship was in the City of God, they were never more than "resident aliens" in the City of Man, and should have been living like that.

That Augustine needed to stress this point is remarkable. Only a generation earlier, Emperor Diocletian had been persecuting Christians ruthlessly. Yet early in the fourth century, Eusebius of Caesarea had hailed Emperor Constantine as the "second David" and declared that "by the express appointment of the same God, two roots of blessing, the Roman Empire and the doctrine of Christian piety, sprang up together for the benefit of mankind."[11] Then in the year 388, when Emperor Theodosius declared the Christian faith the official faith of Rome, the newly built Lateran and Vatican basilicas in Rome could barely cope with the crowds seeking baptism. Christians had swung from being the persecuted to being the favored, and basking in their new favor, they had changed their view of Rome.

Rome was no longer regarded as the antichrist, but as the servant of God and the engine of the advance of the kingdom. Many then believed that as Rome prospered and spread, the kingdom of God would prosper and spread. To those who had espoused such a false Christian triumphalism, the fall of Rome was obviously shattering, and Augustine needed to hammer home the differences between the two cities. The City of God was not the City of Man. The City of Man had fallen. The City of God would endure forever.

There was no such background for the rise of Christendom. There had been no persecution beforehand to provide any contrast between the church and the world, and there was no takeover of a previously great power to tempt anyone to any confused identification. Christendom was "all Christian," and it was new and on the rise. The dark ages were past and the light of the gospel was spreading. Out of the chaos and violence of barbarianism, Christendom had created unity and peace. Out of the long centuries of disorder, Christendom was the expression of a new order. Out of the blood, darkness and death of paganism, Christendom represented a bright new vision of a Christian society. And out of the ashes of the collapsed Roman Empire, Christendom was creating a more than worthy successor: Rome with Christian faith at its heart—the "Holy Roman Empire."

Who could argue with such a vision and such an achievement? Who could challenge such success? Not surprisingly, few did. Indeed, the twelfth-century chronicler Otto von Freising directly echoed St. Augustine, but changed the Bishop of Hippo's ideas fatefully. He wrote, "I have been writing the history not of two cities but, almost, of one, which I call 'Christendom.'"[12] It just happened that he was also the uncle of Frederick Barbarossa, the first king to use the term "Holy Roman Empire."

Only one city, not two? Clearly, such was the success of Christendom that the vision of two cities had been lost. There was only one city now, and it was the City of Man confused with the City of God, which meant in turn that without any clear distinction between the two cities, there was no cultural tension and no prophetic critique at the very moment it was most needed. This lack proved fatal, and what might be called the Lucifer maxim was proved true once again: *The corruption of the best makes for the worst corruption.* (Shakespeare: "Lilies that fester smell far worse than weeds."[13])

My point is not to make a gratuitous attack on medieval Catholicism, for Christendom was a courageous attempt to apply the Christian faith to all of life, and many of its gifts to the Western world, such as the universities and the cathedrals, have been rich and inspiring There have also been too many other periods when the same mistake was repeated all over again. In Germany in the 1930s, the Protestant churches became craven in their failure to confront Adolf Hitler; and in Rwanda in the 1980s, many of the churches were culpably silent in failing to challenge the mounting hatred and tribalism that led to the Rwandan massacre in 1994.

But the early and iconic failure of Christendom highlights some crucial lessons. On the one hand, the lack of prophetic distance and critique meant that Christendom died of an internal poisoning rather like uremic poisoning—when the kidney loses its capacity to get rid of waste and the whole body is poisoned. After all, it was practically impossible for anyone in the late medieval period to secede from the church or to argue with it, as the church's coercive power reached further and further—for example, in the horrible practice of forced baptism for the Jews and in the terrible doctrine that "error has no rights." In 1302, Pope Boniface VIII even issued the bull *Unum Sanctam* in which he laid it down as "necessary to salvation that every human creature be subject to the Roman pontiff."[14] Every creature on earth subject to the pope of Rome? The mind boggles at the arrogance of such totalitarian pretensions.

The nineteenth-century world was quite different from the medieval world, rampantly individualistic rather than closed, but Kierkegaard noted a similar trend at work. As the God of love, God did not want to be loved by whole battalions and nations, or by the millions. His desire was always "the individual in opposition to the others." Yet, as Kierkegaard continued, "Gradually the human race came to itself, and, shrewd as it is, it saw that to do away with Christianity was not practicable—'So let us do it by cunning,' they said. 'We are all Christians, and so Christianity is *eo ipso* abolished.'"[15] When Catholics had been openly intolerant to dissent, Protestants were more subtle, but the poisoning and the lack of prophetic critique were the same.

Besides, that same lack of prophetic distance and critique meant that there could be no remedy or counter to the recurring outbreaks of pride, arrogance, evil and hypocrisy. As Kierkegaard observed of the problem of the Protestant church in his own day, "In 'Christendom' we are all Christians—therefore the relationship of opposition drops out. . . . And then (under the name of Christianity) we live a life of paganism."[16] It is no wonder, then, that out of the great "success" of Christendom and the "great age of faith," in both the medieval and the modern ages, came not only magnificent learning, architecture, art and music, but the worst evils ever perpetrated on the world by the Christian church.

There are few parallels to the scale and shame of this grand tragedy, and there is no getting around the fact that it is precisely because of its strengths, and above all its institutional size and its immense power and wealth, that the Catholic tradition has proved so vulnerable to corruption—marked not only by its well-known excesses and evils, but by its gross superstitions over such things as relics, the shamelessness of its buck-raking rackets such as the selling of indulgences, the brutal cramping of the human mind in actions such as *The Syllabus of Errors*, and the deep shame of its sexual abuse and pedophilia more recently.

Will leaders such as Pope Francis provide the prophetic correction and restore the church's humility, so that such vast institutional power will prove the true servant of the gospel and the lasting partner of human freedom? What matters now is a frank recognition of the past and its legacy, from all our traditions, including the fact that European secularity today is the exorbitant price the church is still paying today for such evils in the past. As the French revolutionary cry illustrates, the major reason for deep-dyed aversions of secularism is the corruptions of the Christian church in European history—"We must strangle the last king with the guts of the last priest."

The same lesson raises its voice at many humbler levels in the successes both of individual Christians and of churches and spiritual movements. American Evangelicals, for example, basked briefly in the cultural sun after the collapse of Protestant liberalism in the 1960s, flexing their newfound political muscles and enjoying a surge of cultural attention when around a third of America claimed to be "born again"—only to squander the moment with what was commonly their truth-deficient "feel good" theology, sub-Christian politics, mindless evangelism, and a host of trendy chases after relevance that proved transient, worldly and unimpressive. Tellingly, the era of Evangelical prominence coincided with an era of moral degeneration in the nation, which it did nothing to halt. The movement has ended not surprisingly in, first, a suicidal dilution of the Christian faith, and, then, in a significant defection from the faith by those who were repulsed by such shallowness and folly.

Times of success always carry the seeds of the greatest failures. The City of God must always provide a prophetic critique for the City of Man. As the Old Testament shows clearly, prophets themselves need prophets, for even prophets can be corrupted and become false prophets who serve only the status quo and the spirit of the times in which they live. If even the Roman conquerors were wise enough to have a slave to whisper in their ears, "Remember that you are a mortal man," how much more should men and women of God know their need of what John Donne called "eagle-sighted prophets" and their accountability.[17] It is always a double-edged privilege to be crowned with the blessings of success, power, wealth and adulation in this life.

JUST BEFORE DAWN

History's second paradoxical lesson is that *the darkest hour is truly just before dawn.* This of course is the story and the lesson of every revival. Five minutes before the revival breaks out, the spiritual landscape may look dark and bleak, but five minutes later all has changed. As in the prophet Ezekiel's vision, one moment the valley is covered with bones, dead, motionless and "very dry." But the next moment there is a rustling and rattling, and within seconds a mighty army of warriors is rising to take their stand, brought to life by the breath of God through the word of the prophet.

On the one hand, our only human contribution to revival is our need and the urgent plea for revival in which our need finds its voice. On the other hand, the power is unmistakably God's power. "Can these bones live?" the Lord asks the prophet, and Ezekiel can only answer, "O Lord GOD, You know."[18] There are many things we humans can do, and unquestionably there are more such things in this generation than in any before us. But life from death, and spiritual life from worldliness and corruption? That is simply beyond us. If it is to be done, only God can do it—and God has, again and again, all down the running centuries.

Thomas Jefferson was a deist, with a highbrow Enlightenment disdain for the supernatural and all who held it central to their

Christian faith. He therefore took great pleasure toward the end of the eighteenth century in predicting the demise of Evangelicalism in America and the triumph of Unitarianism. But brilliant though Jefferson was, his thinking was all "under the sun," and he never took into account any factors beyond the natural. He therefore overlooked the possibility of the supernatural reality of true revival, and he must have been deeply chagrined when the Second Great Awakening led to the resurgence of Evangelicalism and the near demise of Unitarianism.

Even much of our Christian thinking today is like Jefferson's. It is all "under the sun," with the latest sociological statistics and the most incisive commentary, yet it is utterly foolish if it leaves out the only factor that counts in the end—God himself. Armed with batteries of statistics, some startling, some grim, and most of them impeccably accurate, the gloomsters and doomsayers meet us with their worried estimates and their bleak conclusions. "Is it all over?" some ask, confusing the failures of the church and the setbacks to Christian political hopes with the failure of the kingdom itself. "Are we all going the way of Europe?" others wonder, as if there could be no return to God in Europe, and as if Europe had not been lost before and then won back again to faith in Christ.

At the heart of our faith is the glory of the resurrection of Jesus. The same God who brought the universe into being out of nothing and "calls into being that which does not exist"[19] is the God who gives life to the dead and makes the dry bones live. There is a moment when all our "under the sun" estimates appear both realistic and persuasive, and we should never be other than realistic. But then, when God speaks and acts, everything is changed and nothing is the same. With the glory of the resurrection at the center of our faith, and the long story of the church's decline and renewal behind us, it is no cliché but a conviction that the darkest hour is just before the dawn.

FORWARD BEST, BACK FIRST

History's third paradoxical lesson is that *the church always goes forward best by going back first.* If the previous paradox is in danger of being overlooked as a mere cliché, this one runs the risk of open rejection, for it flies squarely into the prevailing winds of modern thinking.

Throughout most of history, most people have been aware of the three faces of time—the past, the present and the future. But the only one they could speak of with any certainty was the past. It had happened. It was, as it were, "in the can," and it could not be changed—except for the fact that historians had an annoying habit of changing the interpretation of what everybody thought they knew. But beyond the circles of their own small worlds in villages and small towns, most people knew little of the present in other parts of the world, and they knew nothing of the future.

Our advanced modern speed and "fast-life" have changed all this. We move so fast that we have little time to think of the past. And now, with our "instant total information" we can see everything in the whole world "as it happens," or we can follow it on our up-to-the-minute, round-the-clock news coverage. And most amazingly, through the wonders of the crystal ball of (the quack science of) futurism, we now know the future too—or presume that we do.

The effect of the impact of our modern fast-life is to alter our awareness of time and to shift our thinking from the past to the future, and in particular to that speeding instant when the future becomes the present. Miss that moment and you are instantly a loser and an also-ran. But seize that vital, fleeting moment and you have in your hands the magic key to relevance, to power and to success—whether you are launching a political initiative, marketing a product, promoting a message or spreading the news of the kingdom.

That is the secret hold of "the tyranny of the urgent now" and the global resurgence of *carpe diem*. What matters supremely, we are told, is "round-the-clock" awareness and "up-to-the-minute" relevance. Everyone who would be someone has to be constantly up to date, and there is no shame worse than being found out to be "so yesterday," and then "left behind." For those who are mesmerized by such a mindset, desperate never to be found on "the wrong side of history," the urgent will have drowned out the important, "the latest will of course be the greatest," and "the newer the truer," or so it is suggested endlessly.

There are numerous perils in this prevalent modern obsession, not least that it is a recipe for shortsightedness, trendiness, transience and instant obsolescence. But for followers of Jesus, there is also a more fundamental flaw. It is not the way of the kingdom. As the Scriptures and history show beyond a doubt in the long story of restorations and renewals, *the church always goes forward best by going back first.*

This principle is highly unfashionable and it certainly sounds counterintuitive. It courts the danger of being dismissed as "reactionary" and "backward looking," or worse, that it is "not on the right side of history," and therefore cannot possibly be the "wave of the future" and the philosophy of those who fancy themselves as the self-professed "emerging ones," the "vanguard" of the future and the truly "progressive thinkers." Such criticisms are fashionable and hard to shake off, but they miss the genius of the Christian way.

Today's world is pulled between two extremes in many areas, such as the seesaw struggle between individualism and collectivism or corporatism. When it comes to our understanding of time, the two extremes are progressivism versus primitivism, and unquestionably the latter is as bad as the former—whether it takes the form of Muslim Salafism or any other religious fundamentalism that is a forlorn attempt to recover a long lost past.

But when we say that the church goes forward best by going back first, we are not hankering after primitivism or any earlier period. We are talking about a return to God, not an era. Having turned away from God and toward an idol, we are turning away from the idol and back to God. And as the Hebrew Scriptures make clear, such a "return" is never reactionary. We are talking of going back to a person and not a period, to God and not to a golden age.

There would be no point in going back to the era of the first-century church. It was no golden age, and the New Testament is frank in recording the errors, prejudices, scandals, corruptions and divisions of the first followers of Jesus. Peter was prejudiced against Gentiles, Ananias and Sapphira were liars, the Christians in Corinth were as loose in their morals as the pagans in the city around them, and so it goes. These first followers of Jesus were "saints" in the new Christian sense of the word, but they were anything but "saintly" in the meaning the word has come to have.

To be sure, we may observe several things in the early church that we have forgotten, distorted or misunderstood to our loss—supremely the position and power of the Holy Spirit—and we should always be quick to learn from them and gain from such rediscoveries. But as a period neither that age, nor any other age before our own, is the decisive model or standard for us. The only perfect model and the sole decisive standard is Jesus himself—his character, his teaching, his commands and his endorsement of the authority of the Scriptures to his followers.

Will we have differences of interpretation as to who Jesus is and what he meant? Of course. Will there be odd, extreme and even false applications of what he said and meant, and what the

Scriptures teach? Beyond a doubt. But our views and interpretations are not authoritative. The sole decisive authority is not that of any infallible leader, for there is no such person. Nor is it that of any group. The supreme and sole authority is Jesus himself, his announcement of the good news of the kingdom of God that is breaking in, and his demonstration of the sole and final authority of the Scriptures. It is this evangelical standard and this evangelical authority that stands over all our beliefs and formulations as the ultimate standard, model and corrective of all we think and do.

In that profound sense, recognizing that we are all more sinful and more culturally shortsighted than we realize, we acknowledge the evangelical imperative. The evangelical imperative is the requirement that confronts all followers of Jesus, from the humblest layperson to the most brilliant scholar to the loftiest archbishop and megachurch pastor: *We are called to define our faith, our lives and all we are and think and do by the standard of Jesus Christ our Lord, the precepts of the good news of the kingdom, and the authority of the Holy Scriptures.*

Thus we are not "primitivists" in the modern sense, but we are not "progressives" in the modern sense either. We only go back to a person and not to a period, so we are able to go forward in any period with no earlier period holding us back. For once again there is no golden age behind us, and the people of every age are as near and dear to God as the people of any other. So the task of Christians in every generation is to be like King David and serve God's purpose in their own generation—always moving forward with our God who is always on the move.

The new wine of the kingdom always requires new wineskins, and it is no accident that when Christians move with the Spirit of God, the Christian faith becomes the most progressive faith in history—though, and here is the crucial difference from modern progressivism, the Christian faith always has a standard by which to assess the purported progress. Once again, the evangelical imperative and the evangelical standard are decisive. Every self-professed Christian life and everything purportedly Christian in the church's thinking and action has to pass the searching assessment of the authority of Jesus, his announcement of the kingdom and the authority of the Scriptures that he endorsed.

Without such a standard by which to measure it, progressivism means nothing, for progress means progress only if there is a destination and some measurable movement toward it. How else would there be any progression at all? So-called progressivism often turns out to be empty and goes nowhere. Progressives all too easily become reactionaries, and the constant craze for relevance is a surefire way of spinning wheels. Certain extremes of Protestant liberalism have abandoned any pretense of submitting to the evangelical imperative and are demonstrating the age-old folly of empty progressives all over again. Progressives may even go backward, whereas "going forward by going back first" is the secret of true and measurable progress.

Does the maxim still sound reactionary? Once, after Dr. Billy Graham had returned from preaching in the Soviet Union, he was roundly criticized by a liberal churchman for the simplicity of his message. "Dr. Graham has set the church back fifty years," the liberal harrumphed.

Hearing the criticism, Billy answered quietly, "I wish I could have set the church back two thousand years!"

Two of the most influential and progressive movements in Western history were the Renaissance and the Reformation. Between them they have been praised and blamed for creating the modern world, yet they were both radical in the sense of going back to the roots and in being movements of recovery—the Renaissance going back to recover the roots of classical learning, and the Reformation going back to recover the gospel of Jesus and the message of the Scriptures.

Needless to say, our golden age is ahead and all the ages behind us have their flaws, so this is not an argument for an uncritical espousal of the Reformation or any other period. Rather it is a call for constant reformation itself, and in particular for the principle of *semper reformanda.* "No God but God," it was once said, and "Nothing is sacred but the sacred" (*nihil mihi sacrum nisi sacrum*). But what those radical imperatives mean is that we must challenge all that is commonly accepted, refuse to be beguiled by the apparently self-evident and the merely traditional, and be prepared to stand perpetually restless before the face of complacency.

Put differently, the defining affirmation of faith for the Christian as a follower of Jesus is that "Jesus is Lord." The evangelical imperative is therefore that every article of faith, every assumption of thought, every Christian practice, and every Christian habit and tradition pass muster under the searching scrutiny of what Jesus announced and initiated in the coming of his kingdom.

It was that standard that showed much of the Renaissance church as corrupt, worldly and anything but Christian, and it is that standard that exposes many of the modern churches in the Western world as more modern than Christian.

Our golden age beckons us from ahead, but in fact the three faces of time break down before the lordship of Jesus. It appears that the gold standard for our faith lies in the past—though not in the first century itself, and not in the early church, but in Jesus himself and the supreme, decisive authority of his lordship, his call and his commands in the Gospels. But precisely because it is Jesus and not a period in the past, that past is not simply the past, but a past made present. For the Jesus who speaks to us from the record of the Gospels and the New Testament is also our contemporary through the power of his Spirit, promised and sent by him to be his presence with us now. He is yesterday, today and forever.

Thus in this generation as in every generation, we all often go wrong, and it is always time to go back to him in order to go forward and on with God.

A Prayer

Lord of the years, sovereign over time and history, speak to us in power by your Word and Spirit, and so break into the short-sightedness and errors of our understanding. Help us to distinguish the true from the false, the enduring from the passing, and the costly from the cheap. Grant us the courage to be faithful rather than fashionable, and turn our eyes from the quicksands of nostalgia and the mirage of an imaginary future. Give to us such a clear understanding of the times in which we live that we may serve your purposes in our generation and be more truly your people in our world today. In the name of Jesus, Amen.

Questions for Discussion

1. Think about your greatest Christian heroes or your favorite period of Christian history, and draw up a ledger of their best and worst features. What does it mean to say our golden age is always ahead?

2. As you look at the situation of the church in the Western world, are you inclined toward discouragement or toward

hope? Is the possibility of renewal and revival a living reality for you and most Christians you know?

3. How does the Christian faith avoid the twin perils of primitivism and progressivism? As you look at the church now, where do you think we need to "go back to go forward" today?

CONCLUDING POSTSCRIPT

One More Time Again?

After we have explored the swirling issues outlined here, the urgent questions facing us are plain. We might look back over the fiascoes and failures of two thousand years and ask what we Christians have done with the great heritage that is ours, but that way leads too often to nostalgia and despair. Our pressing questions must be more immediate and more loyal to our Lord.

Another set of questions stems from the natural thought: What next? On the one hand, we might answer that question by tracing the arc of history as seen from the perspective of Europe's Eastern Orthodox Christians. Seen this way, the faith has moved from Jerusalem to Rome, and then under Emperor Constantine to the "Second Rome" (Constantinople) and then, after the siege of Constantinople and the triumph of the Turks in 1452, to the "Third Rome" (Moscow). Yet for all their strengths, the Eastern churches, in both their Greek and Russian forms, have experienced so many corruptions and committed so many oppressions along the way that the reaction to them has also helped to produce the most antireligious tyranny in history (Soviet communism) and then the troubling authoritarianism of its successor (the Russian regime of Vladimir Putin). The present need for reformation and revival among Europe's Eastern Christians is all too plain.

Looked at from the perspective of Europe's Western Christians, the faith has moved from Jerusalem to Rome, and then, through the conversion of the barbarian peoples, to the center and north of Europe, and then—after the tragic secularization, corruption and division of the church—the Roman Catholics led the expansion of the church to South America and to the achievements of the Baroque renaissance, just as the Protestant branches of the church led a historic expansion to the wider West of the United States, Canada, Australia and New Zealand, and to missionary outreaches from there to the whole world.

Through these efforts of the Western church, both Roman Catholic and Protestant, the gospel has now reached the furthest ends of the entire world, and the Christian faith is the world's first truly global religion. Yet in the process, and due directly to her flaws and failures, the Western church has triggered vehement reactions against itself. These have led to the creation of societies that are more secular than any previous societies in history, and a way of life without God that has marginalized the church herself and reduced it to irrelevance in many modern countries. The urgent need for reformation and revival in both branches of the Western church is equally plain.

There are further questions that grow out of this situation in turn—above all, can Western civilization endure if the Jewish and Christian faiths that were its strongest foundation are removed from influence altogether? Can post-Christian secular faiths provide the grounding for notions such as human dignity, individual liberty, personal responsibility and human sexuality, which were the gifts of the gospel to the West and are crucial to Western freedoms? Or are proud Western boasts about freedom and democracy about to be drowned, not in the hard despotisms of post-Christian Nazism and Communism, but in the soft despotism of the post-Christian centralized, bureaucratic, all-encompassing and government-heavy societies toward which we are fast sliding now? What is certain is that if the Christian faith fails to recover its integrity and cultural influence, post-Christian secularism will be in control, and this time it will have no alibi. All that ensues for the West will be the responsibility of our brave new godless self-gods.

For the purposes of this book, that question about saving us from ourselves must wait for another day. What matters here are questions that concern the Christian faith and the church directly. The deepest question concerns the Lord himself: Is it really conceivable that God will revive the Western church a third time, after it has gone cold twice? Another question concerns our response: What are we to do as we wait for God's answer to that first titanic question? In other words, our deepest questions at this moment echo the very question God asked of the prophet Ezekiel as he surveyed a valley full of the sun-bleached bones of a defeated and slaughtered army, "Can these bones live?"

And like Ezekiel, our answer can only be, "O Lord, you know."[1]

BECAUSE HE CAN

The answer to the second question is the clearer. Acknowledging the essential part that only God can play should never lead to quietism or passivity. We may contribute little to our own renewal except the needs that make our renewal necessary, but to return to Christ in repentance is to shoulder our full responsibilities as disciples—including our commitment to engage to the fullest extent our callings in the world, and our dedication to re-evangelize the advanced modern world. For whether the times are bright or dark, whether we can see God in action in front of us or he seems absent and long delayed, and whether our cultural standing is once again admired or disdainfully cold-shouldered, we have our trust in him to be true to, our tasks to perform and our callings to which we must prove faithful.

As always, faithfulness is all, and the circumstances are beside the point. Our faithfulness must therefore show itself in a waiting that is vigilant, energetic and enterprising. Wherever there are men and women faithful to the Lord, let them trust God and live out their calling to Jesus and their callings in the world wherever those callings take them. That is the call to faithfulness and active transforming engagement that we pray will flower in a new Christian renaissance in our time.

Much of the recent debate about changing the world sounded like a clash between those who say, "Yes, we can," and those who say, "No, you can't." That at least is an issue that can be resolved. The true answer is one we must both declare and live out: Yes, we can, because God can—and he has in the past, and he is doing so elsewhere in the world, and he is able to do so again even here in the advanced modern world, because God is God, and his is the last word in human affairs.

Let it be clearly understood that our hope in the possibility of renewal is squarely grounded, not in ourselves, not in history and the fact that it has happened before, but in the power of God demonstrated by the truth of the resurrection of Jesus. Ever since humans have reflected on the meaning of life in the face of death, we have raised our variations on the question, "Can these bones live?" or "If a man die, shall he live again?" In *Antigone*, for example, Sophocles's great celebration of humanity, he speaks of the human as "clever beyond all dreams," but "there's only death that he cannot find an escape from."[2] We may master nature, we may master each other, and we may sometimes even master ourselves, but we cannot master death.

But Jesus did. Like lightning in the pitch darkness of midnight, his resurrection flashes across the human landscape as the day death died, and the poet John Donne states well the human response now, "Death, be not proud." The risen Jesus stands as the Lord of life, and the lesser challenge of Christian renewal looks puny in the light of the greater triumph of the resurrection of Jesus.

We Christians are weak human vehicles, so our confidence does not lie in ourselves. Our circumstances may be crushingly real, but for us they are never decisive. Jesus warned us of terrors to come that will be far greater than ours today—the prospect of wars, rumors of wars, persecutions, disasters and distress, and times when people would faint for fear. But in his mouth this dire forecast was a call to hope: "Straighten up and lift up your heads, because your redemption is drawing near."[3]

So yes, we can because God can. This is therefore no time to hang our heads or hide our lights under any bushel for fear that we may be picked on for our refusal to fit in. We are to have no fear. We are to look up. We are to take strength from the fact that we can, because he can. But how do we think about it and go about it? Like Karl Barth, the great Reformer Martin Luther could be described as like a man climbing the steep, spiral steps of a medieval cathedral tower in the pitch darkness. Afraid of slipping, he reached out in the dark to feel for the stair rope. Finding it, he grasped it in his hand, and pulled on it to steady himself—only to hear a bell ring out above him, which woke up the entire countryside around. He had searched for the stair rope, but found the bell rope.

The Reformation, in other words, did not come then, and our

much needed reformation today will not come, when Christian leaders sit around a board table with yellow pads and outline their vision from "mission" to "measurable outcomes." Rather, it will come when men and women of God wrestle with God as Jacob wrestled with the angel—wrestling with God, with their consciences, with their times and with the state of the church in their times, until out of that intense wrestling comes an experience of God that is shattering and all-decisive, and the source of what may later once again be termed a reformation. "I will not let you go unless you bless me."[4]

NON NOBIS

That answer still leaves the first and bigger question: Will God renew and revive the Western church again, and through it perhaps contribute to a new Western world and a blessing to the whole world? The point would be hotly contested today, but the lessons of history and the observations of some of the world's greatest thinkers would converge on one conclusion. If there is no renewal, it is not only the Western church but the future of the entire Western world that will be called into question.

Christopher Dawson is once again the clearest prophet, demonstrating that those who see the past most clearly are often the ones to see the future best.

This spiritual alienation of its own greatest minds is the price that every civilization has to pay when it loses its religious foundations, and is contented with a purely material success. We are only just beginning to understand how intimately and profoundly the vitality of a society is bound up with its religion. It is the religious impulse which supplies the cohesive force which unifies a society and a culture. The great civilizations of the world do not produce the great religions as a kind of cultural by-product; in a very real sense, the great religions are the foundations on which the great civilizations rest. A society which has lost its religion becomes sooner or later a society which has lost its culture.[5]

In the debate after World War II, which I have repeatedly engaged at many points rather than referring only to current thinkers, some of the contributors were not so sure of a positive outcome. Emil Brunner, the Swiss theologian expressed his doubts openly as he began his contribution in the Gifford Lectures. "Sometimes I even think it is already too late."[6] Dawson, the eminent historian, was not so hesitant. He raised our precise question, and answered clearly in the affirmative. But as he did so, he stressed the seriousness of the question as well as the gravity of the answer we must give.

Can this miracle be repeated in a world that has for the second time grown cold? Can the Word of Life once more enlighten the darkness of a civilization that is infinitely richer and more powerful than that of pagan Rome but which seems equally to have lost its sense of direction and to be threatened with social degeneration and spiritual disintegration?

It is obvious that the Christian must answer in the affirmative. Yet on the other hand he must not look for a quick and easy solution to a problem on which the whole future of humanity depends.[7]

Those last ten words should give us pause as we come to the end of this brief but important conversation. We began with a twentieth-century battle that was pronounced decisive for the survival of Christian civilization, and we end with the possibility of a revival of the Christian faith pronounced decisive for the survival of humanity. There is no missing the fact that the stakes are high, the urgency is great, and the gravity is plain. We are entering a crunch generation for the world. The global era is raising questions for humanity that are unprecedented and that will call into question the very future of humankind and of our planet home. Much of the world as Christians have known it for centuries has gone, and what the world of tomorrow will be like we do not know and we cannot see.

But those who know and trust God need not fear. The recovery of the integrity and effectiveness of faith in the advanced modern world is a titanic task that boggles the mind and daunts the heart. But God is greater than all, so God may be trusted in all situations. The time has come to trust God, move out, sharing and demonstrating the good news, following his call and living out our callings in every area of our lives, and then leave the outcome to him.

Transforming engagement in the power of the gospel will never prove vain. Living-in-truth is bound to create irresistible consequences. Will such active obedience lead to an astonishing spiritual renaissance, or will the next generation of the church on the earth have to remain faithful through a new dark age, or through times that are something in between?

Once again, "O Lord, you know."

We wait for God's answer, but as we wait, we work. We may be in the dark about our times, but we are not in the dark about God. Whatever the future holds, we are walking in the light with our Lord, so followers of Jesus must have the courage and the faith to work for a new renaissance in our time. So let there be no fear, nor alarmism, nor despondency, nor nostalgia. Instead, let us look up and so act with faith as to say with our prayers as with our lives, "Let a thousand flowers bloom!" And then let us care nothing for any fashionable talk of legacy, but leave the outcome of our enterprise to God and to history.

And as ever, *non nobis*. "Not to us, O LORD, not to us, but to Your name give glory."[8]

A Prayer

"O God, restore us, and cause your face to shine *upon us*, and we will be saved."[9]

O God of life and power, at whose voice our universe sprang into being, and through whose power even death could not hold Jesus down, we worship you as the victor over death, the healer of disease, the reverser of decline and the reformer of corruption. Hear our prayer. Have mercy on our sorry state. Do not leave us to the consequences of our choices, but by your grace forgive our sins, visit us again in our helplessness, and bring to us a new springtime of truth, justice, freedom and peace for our world—not for our sake, O Lord, but for the honor and glory of your matchless name throughout the earth. In the name of Jesus, Amen.

Questions for Discussion

1. What part does prayer for revival play in your life and in the life of your church?

2. Some of King David's men were described as being "skilled in reading the signs of the times, to know what course Israel should follow."[10] Regardless of whether you agree with the argument of this book, outline the contours of the "signs of the times," as you see them, and what they mean for your understanding of faith at this moment in history.

3. Ponder and discuss with your closest Christian friends how your gifts and calling in your part of the world might contribute to an overall spiritual and cultural renaissance in our time.

INTRODUCTION TO
AN EVANGELICAL MANIFESTO

The Evangelical Manifesto was published in Washington,
DC, in May 2008, to reaffirm the foundational importance of the evangelical principle and imperative in the
Christian faith and for all Christians, but especially for those
who identify themselves within the Evangelical movement, or
Evangelicalism.[1] I was among those drafting and signing this
manifesto, most of whom were American Evangelicals, but
anyone reading it can see that its import goes far beyond any
one nation and time.

All who are concerned for the evangelical principle and imperative are confronted with a grand irony today. On the one
hand, the terms *evangelical* and *Evangelicals* are widely derided
or dismissed today because they have become laden with cultural and political baggage, so much so that many are abandoning both the terms and the movement. The manifesto grew
in part from the widespread concern that "evangelical" and
"Evangelical" were too important to allow them to be confused

with political and cultural labels, and therefore that a positive statement was needed to counter this erroneous impression.

On the other hand, many people in other traditions of the Christian faith are increasingly recognizing the inescapable importance of reintroducing the evangelical principle into their own understanding of the faith, and therefore speaking of an "evangelical Catholicism," an "evangelical Orthodoxy," and so on.

The lessons of this irony are plain. The evangelical principle and the evangelical imperative lie at the heart of the Christian faith, and they must never be abandoned. They are part of "the plain, central Christianity" that C. S. Lewis, following Richard Baxter, called "mere Christianity."[2] But they are essentially theological terms, so they must never be confused with any purely human movement, let alone be laden with the political and cultural baggage of any passing generation.

The Evangelical Manifesto therefore reaffirms the primary spiritual and theological significance of "evangelical," and asserts that, properly understood, the principle and the imperative are nonnegotiable in understanding and expressing the good news of Jesus, in living the Christian faith and in reforming the church when it has grown worldly and corrupt. It is significant that the term *Protestant* was invented by the Counter Reformation as a term of abuse. The truth is that the Reformers in the sixteenth century were called "Evangelicals" before they were called "Protestants." "Evangelical" spoke of what they were seeking to return to. In 1536, when the General Assembly of the City of Geneva voted to join with Bern and the Reformation, they voted to "Live by the Gospel." Earlier, when Francis of Assisi determined to live closer to the way of Jesus in his daily life, he too was praised by the pope of his day for being "evangelical." Even earlier still, the prophet Isaiah was hailed rightly as the "evangelical prophet."

In other words, the deeper into history we go, the less sufficient all other labels are. They are shown up as the product of one age or another, and they do not go all the way back to Jesus himself. Catholics often say that to go deep in history is to go beyond Protestantism, and they are right, for Protestantism is a term limited by its times. But to go deep in history is also to go beyond Catholicism and Orthodoxy too, for those labels do not go all the way back to the authority and standard of Jesus. In short, the Evangelical movement itself is recent, whether it is traced back to the Reformation or the First Great Awakening in the eighteenth century, and in many ways the movement is in danger of losing touch with its core principle. But its core principle is synonymous with the gospel itself. There is therefore no substitute for the evangelical principle and imperative, properly understood. There never will be, and there never can be. They are not an alien growth on the great tree of faith with its many branches, but part of the very sap and trunk of the tree.

As long as there are followers of Jesus Christ on earth, there will always be people who understand this truth clearly: Whatever the defining issues in any generation, there is no more authoritative definition of the Christian faith, Christian thinking and the Christian way of life than the supreme standard of Jesus himself, the good news of the kingdom of God that he announced, taught, demonstrated and advanced, including the supreme authority of the Scriptures that he endorsed and the power of the Spirit whom he sent. No other authorities are ever infallible. All must be subject to the supreme and final authority of the Word and the Spirit, the whole of the Word and the Spirit, and nothing less than the Word and the Spirit.

St. Athanasius and St. Augustine lived more than a millennium before the Reformation, but it was their view that the entire Christian era is the age of re-creation and reformation.

"What then was God to do?" Athanasius wrote of God's response
to sin as nothing less than "re-creation." "What else could he
possibly do, being God, but renew his image in mankind?"[3] The
Christian era, Augustine wrote, is the age in which "we are reformed to the image of God."[4] Their point is very close to the
principle of *semper reformanda*, though in practice the Reformation principle tends to focus on the negative, the recurring
forms of bondage from which the church needs freeing, whereas
Athanasius and Augustine put the emphasis on the positive—
Jesus himself—into whose likeness we are being transformed as
at the first creation.

But in either case, the challenge goes all the way back to Jesus
himself. Whatever our tradition, we are all both individuals and
members of the worldwide church. And our goal as followers of
Jesus is to grow and be shaped in who we are and how we think
and act, so that we become more and more like Jesus, and live
closer and closer to the way of Jesus, and so are freely able to
invite others to join us in that venture too. Along that way lies
a life of freedom and service for each of us, and along that way
lies the hope of reformation, restoration and renewal for humanity. If there is a correct and understandable call today for
"evangelical Catholics" and "evangelical Orthodox," there is no
less urgent a call for "evangelical Evangelicals." Only as all followers of Jesus are all truly evangelical will we together become
worthy of his great call.

An Evangelical Manifesto

A Declaration of Evangelical Identity
and Public Commitment

Keenly aware of the hour of history in which we live, and of the momentous challenges that face our fellow humans on the earth and our fellow Christians around the world, we who sign this declaration do so as American leaders and members of one of the world's largest and fastest growing movements of the Christian faith: the Evangelicals.

Evangelicals have no supreme leader or official spokesperson, so no one speaks for all Evangelicals, least of all those who claim to. We speak for ourselves, but as a representative group of Evangelicals in America. We gratefully appreciate that our spiritual and historical roots lie outside this country, that the great majority of our fellow-Evangelicals are in the Global South rather than the North, and that we have recently had a fresh infusion of Evangelicals from Latin America,

Africa, and Asia. We are therefore a small part of a far greater worldwide movement that is both forward looking and outward reaching. Together with them, we are committed to being true to our faith and thoughtful about our calling in today's world.

The two-fold purpose of this declaration is first to address the confusions and corruptions that attend the term *Evangelical* in the United States and much of the Western world today, and second to clarify where we stand on issues that have caused consternation over Evangelicals in public life.

As followers of "the narrow way," our concern is not for approval and popular esteem. Nor do we regard it as accurate or faithful to pose as victims, or to protest at discrimination. We certainly do not face persecution like our fellow-believers elsewhere in the world. Too many of the problems we face as Evangelicals in the United States are those of our own making. If we protest, our protest has to begin with ourselves.

Rather, we are troubled by the fact that the confusions and corruptions surrounding the term *Evangelical* have grown so deep that the character of what it means has been obscured and its importance lost. Many people outside the movement now doubt that *Evangelical* is ever positive, and many inside now wonder whether the term any longer serves a useful purpose.

In contrast to such doubts, we boldly declare that, if we make clear what we mean by the term, we are unashamed to be Evangelical and Evangelicals. We believe that the term is important because the truth it conveys is all-important. A proper understanding of *Evangelical* and the Evangelicals has its own contribution to make, not only to the church but to the wider world; and especially to the plight of many who are poor, vulnerable, or without a voice in their communities.

HERE WE STAND, AND WHY IT MATTERS

This manifesto is a public declaration, addressed both to our fellow-believers and to the wider world. To affirm who we are and where we stand in public is important because we Evangelicals in America, along with people of all faiths and ideologies, represent one of the greatest challenges of the global era: living with our deepest differences. This challenge is especially sharp when religious and ideological differences are ultimate and irreducible, and when the differences are not just between personal worldviews but between entire ways of life co-existing in the same society.

The place of religion in human life is deeply consequential. Nothing is more natural and necessary than the human search for meaning and belonging, for making sense of the world and finding security in life. When this search is accompanied by the right of freedom of conscience, it issues in a freely chosen diversity of faiths and ways of life, some religious and transcendent, and some secular and naturalistic.

Nevertheless, the different faiths and the different families of faith provide very different answers to life, and these differences are decisive not only for individuals but for societies and entire civilizations. Learning to live with our deepest differences is therefore of great consequence both for individuals and nations. Debate, deliberation, and decisions about what this means for our common life are crucial and unavoidable. The alternative— the coercions of tyranny or the terrible convulsions of Nietzsche's "wars of spirit"—would be unthinkable.

We ourselves are those who have come to believe that Jesus of Nazareth is "the way, the truth, and the life," and that the great change required of those who follow him entails a radically new view of human life and a decisively different way of living, thinking, and acting.

Our purpose here is to make a clear statement to our fellow-citizens and our fellow-believers alike, whether they see themselves as our friends, bystanders, skeptics, or enemies. We wish to state what we mean by *Evangelical*, and what being Evangelicals means for our life alongside our fellow citizens in public life and our fellow humans on the earth today. We see three major mandates for Evangelicals.

1. We Must Reaffirm Our Identity

Our first task is to reaffirm who we are. *Evangelicals are Christians who define themselves, their faith, and their lives according to the Good News of Jesus of Nazareth.* (*Evangelical* comes from the Greek word for *good news,* or *gospel.*) Believing that the Gospel of Jesus is God's good news for the whole world, we affirm with the Apostle Paul that we are "not ashamed of the gospel of Jesus Christ, for it is the power of God unto salvation." Contrary to widespread misunderstanding today, we Evangelicals should be defined theologically, and not politically, socially, or culturally.

Behind this affirmation is the awareness that identity is powerful and precious to groups as well as to individuals. Identity is central to a classical liberal understanding of freedom. There are grave dangers in identity politics, but we insist that we ourselves, and not scholars, the press, or public opinion, have the right to say who we understand ourselves to be. We are who we say we are, and we resist all attempts to explain us in terms of our "true" motives and our "real" agenda.

Defined and understood in this way, Evangelicals form one of the great traditions that have developed within the Christian Church over the centuries. We fully appreciate the defining principles of other major traditions, and we stand and work with them on many ethical and social issues of common concern. Like them, we are whole-heartedly committed to the priority of "right belief and right worship," to the "universality" of the Christian church across the centuries, continents, and cultures, and therefore to the central axioms of Christian faith expressed in the Trinitarian and Christological consensus of the early church. Yet we hold to Evangelical beliefs that are distinct from the other traditions in important ways—distinctions that we affirm because we see them as biblical truths that were recovered by the Protestant Reformation, sustained in many subsequent movements of revival and renewal, and vital for a sure and saving knowledge of God—in short, beliefs that are true to the Good News of Jesus.

Evangelicals are therefore followers of Jesus Christ, plain ordinary Christians in the classic and historic sense over the last two thousand years. Evangelicals are committed to thinking, acting, and living as Jesus lived and taught, and so to embody this truth and his Good News for the world that we may be recognizably his disciples. The heart of the matter for us as Evangelicals is our desire and commitment, in the words of Richard of Chichester and as Scripture teaches, to "see him more clearly, to love him more dearly, and to follow him more nearly."

We do not claim that the Evangelical principle—to define our faith and our life by the Good News of Jesus—is unique to us. Our purpose is not to attack or to exclude but to remind and to reaffirm, and so to rally and to reform. For us it is the defining imperative and supreme goal of all who would follow the way of Jesus.

Equally, we do not typically lead with the name *Evangelical* in public. We are simply Christians, or followers of Jesus, or adherents of "mere Christianity," but the Evangelical principle is at the heart of how we see and live our faith.

This is easy to say but challenging to live by. To be Evangelical, and to define our faith and our lives by the Good News of Jesus as taught in Scripture, is to submit our lives entirely to the lordship of Jesus and to the truths and the way of life that he requires of his followers, in order that they might become like him, live the way he taught, and believe as he believed. As Evangelicals have pursued this vision over the centuries, they have prized above all certain beliefs that we consider to be at the heart of the message of Jesus and therefore foundational for us—the following seven above all:

First, we believe that Jesus Christ is fully God become fully human, the unique, sure, and sufficient revelation of the very being, character, and purposes of God, beside whom there is no other god, and beside whom there is no other name by which we must be saved.

Second, we believe that the only ground for our acceptance by God is what Jesus Christ did on the cross and what he is now doing through his risen life, whereby he exposed and reversed the course of human sin and violence, bore the penalty for our sins, credited us with his righteousness, redeemed us from the power of evil, reconciled us to God, and empowers us with his life "from above." We therefore bring nothing to our salvation. Credited with the righteousness of Christ, we receive his redemption solely by grace through faith.

Third, we believe that new life, given supernaturally through spiritual regeneration, is a necessity as well as a gift; and that the lifelong conversion that results is the only pathway to a radically changed character and way of life. Thus for us, the only sufficient power for a life of Christian faithfulness and moral integrity in this world is that of Christ's resurrection and the power of the Holy Spirit.

Fourth, we believe that Jesus' own teaching and his attitude toward the total truthfulness and supreme authority of the Bible, God's inspired Word, make the Scriptures our final rule for faith and practice.

Fifth, we believe that being disciples of Jesus means serving him as Lord in every sphere of our lives, secular as well as spiritual, public as well as private, in deeds as well as words, and in every moment of our days on earth, always reaching out as he did to those who are lost as well as to the poor, the sick, the hungry, the oppressed, the socially despised, and being faithful stewards of creation and our fellow-creatures.

Sixth, we believe that the blessed hope of the personal return of Jesus provides both strength and substance to what we are doing, just as what we are doing becomes a sign of the hope of where we are going; both together leading to a consummation of history and the fulfillment of an undying kingdom that comes only by the power of God.

Seventh, we believe all followers of Christ are called to know and love Christ through worship, love Christ's family through fellowship, grow like Christ through discipleship, serve Christ by ministering to the needs of others in his name, and share Christ with those who do not yet know him, inviting people to the ends of the earth and to the end of time to join us as his disciples and followers of his way.

At the same time, we readily acknowledge that we repeatedly fail to live up to our high calling, and all too often illustrate the truth of our own doctrine of sin. We Evangelicals share the same "crooked timber" of our humanity, and the full catalogue of our sins, failures, and hypocrisies. This is no secret either to God or to those who know and watch us.

DEFINING FEATURES

Certain implications follow from this way of defining Evangelicalism:

First, to be Evangelical is to hold a belief that is also a devotion. Evangelicals adhere fully to the Christian faith expressed in the historic creeds of the great ecumenical councils of the church, and in the great affirmations of the Protestant Reformation, and seek to be loyal to this faith passed down from generation to generation. But at its core, being Evangelical is always more than a creedal statement, an institutional affiliation, or a matter of membership in a movement. We have no supreme leader, and neither creeds nor tradition are ultimately decisive for us. Jesus Christ and his written word, the Holy Scriptures, are our supreme authority; and whole-hearted devotion, trust, and obedience are our proper response.

Second, Evangelical belief and devotion is expressed as much in our worship and in our deeds as in our creeds. As the universal popularity of such hymns and songs as "Amazing Grace" attests, our great hymn writers stand alongside our great theologians, and often our commitment can be seen better in our giving and our caring than in official statements. What we are about is captured not only in books or declarations, but in our care for the poor, the homeless, and the orphaned; our outreach to those in prison; our compassion for the hungry and the victims of disaster; and our fight for justice for those oppressed by such evils as slavery and human trafficking.

Third, Evangelicals are followers of Jesus in a way that is not limited to certain churches or contained by a definable movement. We are members of many different churches and denominations, mainline as well as independent, and our Evangelical commitment provides a core of unity that holds together a wide range of diversity. This is highly significant for any movement in the network society of the information age, but Evangelicalism has always been diverse, flexible, adaptable, non-hierarchical, and taken many forms. This is true today more than ever, as witnessed by the variety and vibrancy of Evangelicals around the world. For to be Evangelical is first and foremost a way of being devoted to Jesus Christ, seeking to live in different ages and different cultures as he calls his followers to live.

Fourth, as stressed above, Evangelicalism must be defined theologically and not politically; confessionally and not culturally. Above all else, it is a commitment and devotion to the person and work of Jesus Christ, his teaching and way of life, and an enduring dedication to his lordship above all other earthly powers, allegiances and loyalties. As such, it should not be limited to tribal or national boundaries, or be confused with, or reduced to political categories such as "conservative" and "liberal," or to psychological categories such as "reactionary" or "progressive."

Fifth, the Evangelical message, "good news" by definition, is overwhelmingly positive, and always positive before it is negative. There is an enormous theological and cultural importance to "the power of No," especially in a day when "Everything is permitted" and "It is forbidden to forbid." Just as Jesus did, Evangelicals sometimes have to make strong judgments about what is false, unjust, and evil. But first and foremost we Evangelicals are *for* Someone and *for* something rather than against anyone or anything. The Gospel of Jesus is the Good News of welcome, forgiveness, grace, and liberation from law and legalism. It is a colossal Yes to life and human aspirations, and an emphatic No only to what contradicts our true destiny as human beings made in the image of God.

Sixth, Evangelicalism should be distinguished from two opposite tendencies to which Protestantism has been prone: liberal revisionism and conservative fundamentalism. Called by Jesus to be "in the world, but not of it," Christians, especially in modern society, have been pulled toward two extremes. Those more liberal have tended so to accommodate the world that they reflect the thinking and lifestyles of the day, to the point where they are unfaithful to Christ; whereas those more conservative have tended so to defy the world that they resist it in ways that also become unfaithful to Christ.

The liberal revisionist tendency was first seen in the eighteenth century and has become more pronounced today, reaching a climax in versions of the Christian faith that are characterized by such weaknesses as an exaggerated estimate of human capacities, a shallow view of evil, an inadequate view of truth, and a deficient view of God. In the end, they are sometimes no longer recognizably Christian. As this sorry capitulation occurs, such "alternative gospels" represent a series of severe losses that eventually seal their demise:

First, a loss of authority, as *sola Scriptura* ("by Scripture alone") is replaced by *sola cultura* ("by culture alone");

Second, a loss of community and continuity, as "the faith once delivered" becomes the faith of merely one people and one time, and cuts itself off from believers across the world and down the generations;

Third, a loss of stability, as in Dean Inge's apt phrase, the person "who marries the spirit of the age soon becomes a widower";

Fourth, a loss of credibility, as "the new kind of faith" turns out to be what the skeptic believes already, and there is no longer anything solidly, decisively Christian for seekers to examine and believe;

Fifth, a loss of identity, as the revised version of the faith loses more and more resemblance to the historic Christian faith that is true to Jesus.

In short, for all their purported sincerity and attempts to be relevant, extreme proponents of liberal revisionism run the risk of becoming what Søren Kierkegaard called "kissing Judases"— Christians who betray Jesus with an interpretation.

The fundamentalist tendency is more recent, and even closer to Evangelicalism, so much so that in the eyes of many, the two overlap. We celebrate those in the past for their worthy desire to be true to the fundamentals of faith, but Fundamentalism has become an overlay on the Christian faith and developed into an essentially modern reaction to the modern world. As a reaction to the modern world, it tends to romanticize the past, some now-lost moment in time, and to radicalize the present, with styles of reaction that are personally and publicly militant to the point where they are sub-Christian.

Christian Fundamentalism has its counterparts in many religions and even in secularism, and often becomes a social movement with a Christian identity but severely diminished Christian content and manner. Fundamentalism, for example, all too easily parts company with the Evangelical principle, as can Evangelicals themselves, when they fail to follow the great commandment that we love our neighbors as ourselves, let alone the radical demand of Jesus that his followers forgive without limit and love even their enemies.

Seventh, Evangelicalism is distinctive for the way it looks equally to both the past and the future. In its very essence, Evangelicalism goes back directly to Jesus and the Scriptures, not just as a matter of historical roots, but as a commitment of the heart and as the tenor of its desire and thought; and not just once, but again and again as the vital principle of its way of life. To be Evangelical is therefore not only to be deeply personal in faith, strongly committed to ethical holiness in life, and marked by robust voluntarism in action, but to live out a faith whose dynamism is shaped unashamedly by truth and history.

Yet far from being unquestioning conservatives and unreserved supporters of tradition and the status quo, being Evangelical means an ongoing commitment to Jesus Christ, and this entails innovation, renewal, reformation, and entrepreneurial dynamism, for everything in every age is subject to assessment in the light of Jesus and his Word. The Evangelical principle is therefore a call to self-examination, reflection, and a willingness to be corrected and to change whenever necessary. At the same time, far from being advocates of today's nihilistic "change for change's sake," to be Evangelical is to recognize the primacy of the authority of Scripture, which points us to Jesus, and so to see the need to conserve a form behind all re-form.

We therefore regard reason and faith as allies rather than enemies, and find no contradiction between head and heart, between being fully faithful on the one hand, and fully intellectually critical and contemporary on the other. Thus Evangelicals part company with reactionaries by being both re-forming and innovative, but they also part company with modern progressives by challenging the ideal of the-newer-the-truer and the-latest-is-greatest and by conserving what is true and right and good. For Evangelicals, it is paradoxical though true that the surest way forward is always first to go back, a "turning back" that is the secret of all true revivals and reformations.

In sum, to be Evangelical is earlier and more enduring than to be Protestant. Seeking to be Evangelical was the heart of the Protestant Reformation, and what gives the Reformation its Christian validity for us is its recovery of biblical truth. In some countries *Evangelical* is still synonymous with *Protestant*. Yet it is clear that the term *Evangelical*, and the desire to be biblical, both predate and outlast the Protestant project in its historical form, for the word *protest* has increasingly lost its original positive meaning of "witnessing on behalf of" (*pro-testantes*), and the term *Protestant* is more and more limited to a historical period. Other labels come and go, but the Evangelical principle that seeks to be faithful to the Good News of Jesus and to the Scriptures will always endure.

2. We Must Reform Our Own Behavior

Our second major concern is the reformation of our behavior. We affirm that to be Evangelical or to carry the name *Evangelicals* is not only to shape our faith and our lives according to the teaching and standards of the Way of Jesus, but to need to do so again and again. But if the Evangelical impulse is a radical, reforming, and innovative force, we acknowledge with sorrow a momentous irony today. We who time and again have stood for the renewal of tired forms, for the revival of dead churches, for the warming of cold hearts, for the reformation of corrupt practices and heretical beliefs, and for the reform of gross injustices in society, are ourselves in dire need of reformation and renewal today. Reformers, we ourselves need to be reformed. Protestants, we are the ones against whom protest must be made.

We confess that we Evangelicals have betrayed our beliefs by our behavior.

All too often we have trumpeted the gospel of Jesus, but we have replaced biblical truths with therapeutic techniques, worship with entertainment, discipleship with growth in human potential, church growth with business entrepreneurialism, concern for the church and for the local congregation with expressions of the faith that are churchless and little better than a vapid spirituality, meeting real needs with pandering to felt needs, and mission principles with marketing precepts. In the process we have become known for commercial, diluted, and feel-good gospels of health, wealth, human potential, and religious happy talk, each of which is indistinguishable from the passing fashions of the surrounding world.

All too often we have set out high, clear statements of the authority of the Bible, but flouted them with lives and lifestyles that are shaped more by our own sinful preferences and by modern fashions and convenience.

All too often we have prided ourselves on our orthodoxy, but grown our churches through methods and techniques as worldly as the worldliest of Christian adaptations to passing expressions of the spirit of the age.

All too often we have failed to demonstrate the unity and harmony of the body of Christ, and fallen into factions defined by the accidents of history and sharpened by truth without love, rather than express the truth and grace of the Gospel.

All too often we have traced our roots to powerful movements of spiritual revival and reformation, but we ourselves are often atheists unawares, secularists in practice who live in a world without windows to the supernatural, and often carry on our Christian lives in a manner that has little operational need for God.

All too often we have attacked the evils and injustices of others, such as the killing of the unborn, as well as the heresies and apostasies of theological liberals whose views have developed into "another gospel," while we have condoned our own sins, turned a blind eye to our own vices, and lived captive to forces such as materialism and consumerism in ways that contradict our faith.

All too often we have concentrated on great truths of the Bible, such as the cross of Jesus, but have failed to apply them to other biblical truths, such as creation. In the process we have impoverished ourselves, and supported a culture broadly careless about the stewardship of the earth and negligent of the arts and the creative centers of society.

All too often we have been seduced by the shaping power of the modern world, exchanging a costly grace for convenience, switching from genuine community to an embrace of individualism, softening theological authority down to personal preference, and giving up a clear grasp of truth and an exclusive allegiance to Jesus for a mess of mix-and-match attitudes that are syncretism by another name.

All too often we have disobeyed the great command to love the Lord our God with our hearts, souls, strength, and minds, and have fallen into an unbecoming anti-intellectualism that is a dire cultural handicap as well as a sin. In particular, some among us have betrayed the strong Christian tradition of a high view of science, epitomized in the very matrix of ideas that gave birth to modern science, and made themselves vulnerable to caricatures of the false hostility between science and faith. By doing so, we have unwittingly given comfort to the unbridled scientism and naturalism that are so rampant in our culture today.

All too often we have gloried in the racial and ethnic diversity of the church around the world, but remained content to be enclaves of separateness here at home.

All too often we have abandoned our Lord's concern for those in the shadows, the twilight, and the deep darkness of the world, and become cheerleaders for those in power and the naïve syco-phants of the powerful and the rich.

All too often we have tried to be relevant, but instead of creating "new wineskins for the new wine," we have succumbed to the passing fashions of the moment and made noisy attacks on yesterday's errors, such as modernism, while capitulating tamely to today's, such as postmodernism.

We call humbly but clearly for a restoration of the Evangelical reforming principle, and therefore for deep reformation and renewal in all our Christian ways of life and thought.

We urge our fellow-Evangelicals to go beyond lip-service to Jesus and the Bible and restore these authorities to their supreme place in our thought and practice.

We call our communities to a discerning critique of the world and of our generation, so that we resist not only their obviously alien power but the subtle and seductive shaping of the more brilliant insights and techniques of modernity, remembering always that we are "against the world, for the world."

We call all who follow Jesus to keep his commandment and love one another, to be true to our unity in him that underlies all lesser differences, and to practice first the reconciliation in the church that is so needed in the wider world. In a society divided by identity and gender politics, Christians must witness by their lives to the way their identity in Jesus transcends all such differences.

We call for an expansion of our concern beyond single-issue politics, such as abortion and marriage, and a fuller recognition of the comprehensive causes and concerns of the Gospel, and of all the human issues that must be engaged in public life. Although we cannot back away from our biblically rooted commitment to the sanctity of every human life, including those unborn, nor can we deny the holiness of marriage as instituted by God between one man and one woman, we must follow the model of Jesus, the Prince of Peace, engaging the global giants of conflict, racism, corruption, poverty, pandemic diseases, illiteracy, ignorance, and spiritual emptiness, by promoting reconciliation, encouraging ethical servant leadership, assisting the poor, caring for the sick, and educating the next generation. We believe it is our calling to be good stewards of all God has entrusted to our care so that it may be passed on to generations yet to be born.

We call for a more complete understanding of discipleship that applies faith with integrity to every calling and sphere of life, the secular as well as the spiritual, and the physical as well as the religious; and that thinks wider than politics in contributing to the arts, the sciences, the media, and the creation of culture in all its variety.

Above all, we remind ourselves that if we would recommend the Good News of Jesus to others, we must first be shaped by that Good News ourselves, and thus ourselves be Evangelicals and Evangelical.

3. We Must Rethink Our Place in Public Life

We must find a new understanding of our place in public life. We affirm that to be Evangelical and to carry the name of Christ is to seek to be faithful to the freedom, justice, peace, and well-being that are at the heart of the kingdom of God, to bring these gifts into public life as a service to all, and to work with all who share these ideals and care for the common good. Citizens of the City of God, we are resident aliens in the Earthly City. Called by Jesus to be "in" the world but "not of" the world, we are fully engaged in public affairs, but never completely equated with any party, partisan ideology, economic system, class, tribe, or national identity.

Whereas fundamentalism was thoroughly world-denying and politically disengaged from its outset, names such as John Jay, John Witherspoon, John Woolman, and Frances Willard in America and William Wilberforce and Lord Shaftesbury in England are a reminder of a different tradition. Evangelicals have made a shining contribution to politics in general, to many of the greatest moral and social reforms in history, such as the abolition of slavery and woman's suffrage, and even to notions crucial in political discussion today, for example, the vital but little known Evangelical contribution to the rise of the voluntary association and, through that, to the understanding of such key notions as civil society and social capital.

NEITHER PRIVATIZED NOR POLITICIZED

Today, however, we Evangelicals wish to stand clear from certain positions in public life that are widely confused with Evangelicalism.

First, we Evangelicals repudiate two equal and opposite errors into which many Christians have fallen recently. One error has been to privatize faith, interpreting and applying it to the personal and spiritual realm only. Such dualism falsely divorces the spiritual from the secular, and causes faith to lose its *integrity* and become "privately engaging and publicly irrelevant," and another form of "hot tub spirituality."

The other error, made by both the religious left and the religious right in recent decades, is to politicize faith, using faith to express essentially political points that have lost touch with biblical truth. That way faith loses its *independence*, the church becomes "the regime at prayer," Christians become "useful idiots" for one political party or another, and the Christian faith becomes an ideology in its purest form. Christian beliefs are used as weapons for political interests.

Christians from both sides of the political spectrum, left as well as right, have made the mistake of politicizing faith; and it would be no improvement to respond to a weakening of the religious right with a rejuvenation of the religious left. Whichever side it comes from, a politicized faith is faithless, foolish, and disastrous for the church—and disastrous first and foremost for Christian reasons rather than constitutional reasons.

Called to an allegiance higher than party, ideology, and nationality, we Evangelicals see it our duty to engage with politics, but our equal duty never to be completely equated with any party, partisan ideology, economic system, or nationality. In our scales, spiritual, moral, and social power are as important as political power, what is right outweighs what is popular, just as principle outweighs party, truth matters more than team-playing, and conscience more than power and survival.

The politicization of faith is never a sign of strength but of weakness. The saying is wise: "The first thing to say about politics is that politics is not the first thing."

The Evangelical soul is not for sale. It has already been bought at an infinite price.

A CIVIL RATHER THAN A SACRED OR
A NAKED PUBLIC SQUARE

Second, we Evangelicals repudiate the two extremes that define the present culture wars in the United States. There are deep and important issues at stake in the culture wars, issues on which the future of the United States and Western civilization will turn. But the trouble comes from the manner in which the issues are being fought.

In particular, what we as Evangelicals lament in the culture warring is not just the general collapse of the common vision of the common good, but the endless conflict over the proper place of faiths in public life, and therefore of the freedom to enter and engage public life from the perspective of faith. A grand confusion now reigns as to any guiding principles by which people of different faiths may enter the public square and engage with each other robustly but civilly. The result is the "holy war" front of America's wider culture wars, and a dangerous incubation of conflicts, hatreds, and lawsuits.

We repudiate on one side the partisans of a *sacred public square*, those who for religious, historical, or cultural reasons would continue to give a preferred place in public life to one religion which in almost all most current cases would be the Christian faith, but could equally be another faith. In a society as religiously diverse as America today, no one faith should be normative for the entire society, yet there should be room for the free expression of faith in the public square.

Let it be known unequivocally that we are committed to religious liberty for people of all faiths, including the right to convert to or from the Christian faith. We are firmly opposed to the imposition of theocracy on our pluralistic society. We are also concerned about the illiberalism of politically correct attacks on evangelism. We have no desire to coerce anyone or to impose on anyone beliefs and behavior that we have not persuaded them to adopt freely, and that we do not demonstrate in our own lives, above all by love.

We repudiate on the other side the partisans of a *naked public square*, those who would make all religious expression inviolably private and keep the public square inviolably secular. Often advocated by a loose coalition of secularists, liberals, and supporters of the strict separation of church and state, this position is even less just and workable because it excludes the overwhelming majority of citizens who are still profoundly religious. Nothing is more illiberal than to invite people into the public square but insist that they be stripped of the faith that makes them who they are and shapes the way they see the world.

In contrast to these extremes, our commitment is to a *civil public square—a vision of public life in which citizens of all faiths are free to enter and engage the public square on the basis of their faith, but within a framework of what is agreed to be just and free for other faiths too.* Thus every right we assert for ourselves is at once a right we defend for others. A right for a Christian is a right for a Jew, and a right for a secularist, and a right for a Mormon, and right for a Muslim, and a right for a Scientologist, and right for all the believers in all the faiths across this wide land.

THE WAY OF JESUS, NOT CONSTANTINE

There are two additional concerns we address to the attention of our fellow-citizens. On the one hand, we are especially troubled by the fact that a generation of culture warring, reinforced by understandable reactions to religious extremism around the world, is creating *a powerful backlash against all religion in public life among many educated people.* If this were to harden and become an American equivalent of the long-held European animosity toward religion in the public life, the result would be disastrous for the American republic and a severe constriction of liberty for people of all faiths.

We therefore warn of the striking intolerance evident among the new atheists, and call on all citizens of goodwill and believers of all faiths and none to join with us in working for a civil public square and the restoration of a tough-minded civility that is in the interests of all.

On the other hand, we are also troubled by the fact that the advance of globalization and *the emergence of a global public square finds no matching vision of how we are to live freely, justly, and peacefully with our deepest differences on the global stage.* As the recent Muslim protests and riots over perceived insults to their faith demonstrate, the Internet era has created a world in which everyone can listen to what we say even when we are not intentionally speaking to everyone. The challenges of living with our deepest differences are intensified in the age of global technologies such as the World Wide Web.

As this global public square emerges, we see two equal and opposite errors to avoid: *coercive secularism* on one side, once typified by communism and now by the softer but strict French-style secularism; and *religious extremism* on the other side, typified by Islamist violence.

At the same time, we repudiate the two main positions into which many are now falling. On the one hand, we repudiate those who believe their way is the only way and the way for everyone, and are therefore prepared to coerce others. Whatever the faith or ideology in question, communism, Islam, or even democracy, this position leads inevitably to *conflict*.

Undoubtedly, many people would place all Christians in this category, because of the Emperor Constantine and the state-sponsored oppression he inaugurated, leading to the dangerous alliance between church and state continued in European church-state relations down to the present.

We are not uncritical of unrestrained voluntarism and rampant individualism, but we utterly deplore the dangerous alliance between church and state, and the oppression that was its dark fruit. We Evangelicals trace our heritage, not to Constantine, but to the very different stance of Jesus of Nazareth. While some of us are pacifists and others are advocates of just war, we all believe that Jesus' Good News of justice for the whole world was promoted, not by a conqueror's power and sword, but by a suffering servant emptied of power and ready to die for the ends he came to achieve. Unlike some other religious believers, we do not see insults and attacks on our faith as "offensive" and "blasphemous" in a manner to be defended by law, but as part of the cost of our discipleship that we are to bear without complaint or victim-playing.

On the other hand, we repudiate all who believe that different values are simply relative to different cultures, and who therefore refuse to allow anyone to judge anyone else or any other culture. More tolerant sounding at first, this position leads directly to the evils of *complacency*; for in a world of such evils as genocide, slavery, female oppression, and assaults on the unborn, there are rights that require defending, evils that must be resisted, and interventions into the affairs of others that are morally justifiable.

We also warn of the danger of a *two-tier global public square*, one in which the top tier is for cosmopolitan secular liberals and the second tier is for local religious believers. Such an arrangement would be patronizing as well as a severe restriction of religious liberty and justice, and unworthy of genuine liberalism.

Once again, our choice is for a civil public square, and a working respect for the rights of all, even those with whom we disagree. Contrary to medieval religious leaders and certain contemporary atheists who believe that "error has no rights," we respect the right to be wrong. But we also insist that the principle of "the right to believe anything" does not lead to the conclusion that "anything anyone believes is right." Rather, it means that respect for differences based on conscience can also mean a necessary debate over differences conducted with respect.

INVITATION TO ALL

As stated earlier, we who sign this declaration do not presume to speak for all Evangelicals. *We speak only for ourselves, yet not only to ourselves.* We therefore invite all our fellow-Christians, our fellow-citizens, and people of different faiths across the nation and around the world to take serious note of these declarations and to respond where appropriate.

We urge our fellow-Evangelicals to consider these affirmations and to join us in clarifying the profound confusions surrounding Evangelicalism, that together we may be more faithful to our Lord and to the distinctiveness of his way of life.

We urge our fellow citizens to assess the damaging consequences of the present culture wars, and to work with us in the urgent task of restoring liberty and civility in public life, and so ensure that freedom may last to future generations.

We urge adherents of other faiths around the world to understand that we respect your right to believe what you believe according to the dictates of conscience, and invite you to follow the golden rule and extend the same rights and respect to us and to the adherents of all other faiths, so that together we may make religious liberty practical and religious persecution rarer, so that in turn human diversity may complement rather than contradict human well-being.

We urge those who report and analyze public affairs, such as scholars, journalists, and public policy makers, to abandon stereotypes and adopt definitions and categories in describing us and other believers in terms that are both accurate and fair, and with a tone that you in turn would like to be applied to yourselves.

We urge those in positions of power and authority to appreciate that we seek the welfare of the communities, cities, and countries in which we live, yet our first allegiance is always to a higher loyalty and to standards that call all other standards into question, a commitment that has been a secret of the Christian contributions to civilization as well as its passion for reforms.

We urge those who share our dedication to the poor, the suffering, and the oppressed to join with us in working to bring care, peace, justice, and freedom to those millions of our fellow-humans who are now ignored, oppressed, enslaved, or treated as human waste and wasted humans by the established orders in the global world.

We urge those who search for meaning and belonging amid the chaos of contemporary philosophies and the brokenness and alienation of modern society to consider that the gospel we have found to be good news is in fact the best news ever, and open to all who would come and discover what we now enjoy and would share.

Finally, we solemnly pledge that in a world of lies, hype, and spin, where truth is commonly dismissed and words suffer from severe inflation, we make this declaration in words that have been carefully chosen and weighed; words that, under God, we make our bond. People of the Good News, we desire not just to speak the Good News but to embody and be good news to our world and to our generation.

Here we stand. Unashamed and assured in our own faith, we reach out to people of all other faiths with love, hope, and humility. With God's help, we stand ready with you to face the challenges of our time and to work together for a greater human flourishing.

The End

GRATEFUL ACKNOWLEDGMENTS

My thinking and writing have always sprung from back-of-an-envelope ideas that sprouted and flourished in various settings until they outgrew their scratchy origins. This little book is no exception, and I owe the deepest debt of gratitude to the following friends:

Eric Fellman, Larry Julian and Phil Styrling, whose annual invitation to speak at the business dinner before the National Prayer Breakfast in Washington, DC, has prompted many a new idea and many a later speech.

Tom Tarrants and Kerry Knott, whose invitation to address the annual banquet of the C. S. Lewis Institute in 2011 was the immediate spur to the development of this book. Their friendship, encouragement and partnership go back far earlier and far beyond this book.

Michael Cromartie, Al Hsu, Richard Ohman, Karis Riley, David Wells and an anonymous publisher's reviewer, able and deeply engaged thinkers and good friends whose review of the first draft saved me from several egregious errors and helped to set the book on its present course. Needless to say, I am fully responsible for the final outcome, especially where I may have misunderstood or neglected the better wisdom of their critiques and suggestions.

Al Hsu, Jeff Crosby, Alisse Wissman and all their marvelous colleagues at InterVarsity Press, who make editing and publishing such a pleasure.

Erik Wolgemuth, who is always all and more that a writer wishes an agent to be.

CJ, my son, whose encouragement and support for this particular book have been an inspiration from beginning to end.

And Jenny, my beloved wife and partner, to whom this book is dedicated, whose life, walk of faith and especially her prayer are a model of where many more of us need to go today.

NOTES

CHAPTER 1: OUR AUGUSTINIAN MOMENT

[1]G. K. Chesterton, *The Everlasting Man* (Garden City, NY: Image Books, 1955), pp. 260-61.

[2]Graham Stewart, *His Finest Hours: The War Speeches of Winston Churchill* (London: Quercus, 2007), p. 59.

[3]Friedrich Nietzsche, *The Birth of Tragedy*, trans. Douglas Smith (New York: Oxford University Press, 2000), p. 130; Gerard Manley Hopkins, "God's Grandeur," line 7.

[4]Henry Kissinger, *Does America Need a Foreign Policy? Toward a Diplomacy for the Twenty-First Century* (New York: Simon & Schuster, 2001), p. 17.

[5]Quoted in Christina Scott's foreword to Christopher Dawson, *Progress & Religion* (Washington, DC: Catholic University of America Press, 2001), p. xix.

[6]Søren Kierkegaard, quoted in the supplement to the translator's introduction in *Attack upon "Christendom,"* trans. Walter Lowrie (Princeton, NJ: Princeton University Press, 1968), p. xxxiii.

[7]Christopher Dawson, *Religion and the Rise of Western Culture* (New York: Image Books, 1957), p. 17.

[8]Quoted in Christopher Dawson, *Medieval Essays* (Washington, DC: Catholic University of America Press, 1954), p. 46.

[9]Ibid., p. 28.

[10]Daniel 4:26.

[11]Stewart, *His Finest Hours*, p. 59.

[12]Dawson, *Medieval Essays*, p. 6.

CHAPTER 2: GRAND GLOBAL TASKS

[1]Genesis 12:3.

[2]Matthew 28:19.

[3]See Os Guinness, *The Last Christian on Earth: Discover the Enemy's Plot to Undermine the Church* (Ventura, CA: Regal, 2010).

[4]Romans 12:2.

[5]Walter Lowrie, "Introduction," in Søren Kierkegaard, *Attack upon "Christendom,"* trans. Walter Lowrie (Princeton, NJ: Princeton University Press, 1968), p. xi.

[6]See, for example, David Wells, *No Place for Truth: Or, Whatever Happened to Evangelical Theology* (Grand Rapids: Eerdmans, 1994).

[7]Exodus 23:2.

[8]Quoted in Erik Ritter von Kuehnelt-Leddihn, *Liberty or Equality: The Challenge of Our Time* (Auburn, AL: Ludwig von Mises Institute, 2007), p. 36.

[9]James Fennimore Cooper, *The American Democrat* (New York: Knopf, 1931), p. 64.

[10]John Stuart Mill, "On Liberty," in *On Liberty and the Subjection of Women* (1859; repr., New York: Penguin, 2006), pp. 39-40.

[11]William Edgar and K. Scott Oliphint, eds., *Christian Apologetics Past and Present* (Wheaton, IL: Crossway, 2011), p. 314

[12]Jacob Burckhardt, Letter, September 1866, quoted in Ritter von Kuehnelt Leddihn, *Liberty or Equality,* p. 39.

[13]Kierkegaard, *Attack upon "Christendom,"* p. xxxi.

[14]Seneca, *Letters to Lucilius* 29.10.

[15]See, for example, Richard Fletcher, *The Barbarian Conversion: From Paganism to Christianity* (Berkeley: University of California Press, 1999).

[16]Martin Rees, *Our Final Hour: A Scientist's Warning* (New York: Basic Books, 2004), p. 8.

[17]James Martin, *The Meaning of the 21st Century: A Vital Blueprint for Ensuring Our Future* (New York: Riverhead Books, 2006), p. 19.

[18]See Os Guinness, *The Global Public Square: Religious Freedom and the Making of a World Safe for Diversity* (Downers Grove, IL: InterVarsity Press, 2013).

CHAPTER 3: UNNECESSARY, UNLIKELY, UNDENIABLE

[1]Emil Brunner, *Christianity and Civilisation,* vol. 1, *Foundations* (London: Nisbet & Co., 1948), p. v.

[2]Augustine, *On Christian Doctrine* 2.18, 28.

[3]T. S. Eliot, *Christianity and Culture* (New York: Harcourt, 1976), p. 86.

[4]John 13:34-35.

[5]Tertullian, *On the "Prescription" of Heretics* 7.

[6]From a sermon by James Allan Francis, "Arise, Sir Knight," in *The Real Jesus and Other Sermons* (Valley Forge, PA: Judson Press, 1926).

[7]Christopher Dawson, *Beyond Politics* (New York: Sheed & Ward, 1939), p. 128.

[8]John 8:23.

[9]John 18:36.

[10]Brunner, *Christianity and Civilisation*, p. 6.

[11]Quoted in Robert Hughes, *Rome: A Cultural, Personal, and Visual History* (New York: Knopf, 2011), p. 82.

[12]John Baillie, *What Is Christian Civilization?* (London: Christophers, 1945), p. 69.

CHAPTER 4: THE SECRET OF CULTURAL POWER

[1]C. S. Lewis, "Some Thoughts," in *God in the Dock: Essays on Theology and Ethics* (Grand Rapids: Eerdmans, 2001), p. 147.

[2]Peter L. Berger, "For a World with Windows," in *Against the World for the World*, ed. Peter L. Berger and Richard John Neuhaus (New York: Seabury, 1976), p. 10.

[3]Lewis, "Some Thoughts," p. 147.

[4]Ibid., p. 148.

[5]Matthew Arnold, "Dover Beach," www.poetryfoundation.org/poem/172844.

[6]David Martin, *Dilemmas of Contemporary Religion* (Oxford: Blackwell, 1978), p. 88.

[7]Ibid.

[8]Ibid.

[9]G. K. Chesterton, *The Everlasting Man* (Garden City, NY: Image Books, 1955), pp. 260-61.

[10]John 17:11, 14, 16.

[11]Romans 12:2.

[12]Exodus 11:2; 32:1-35.

[13]T. S. Eliot, *Christianity and Culture* (New York: Harcourt, 1976), p. 72.

[14]John Henry Newman quoted by Christopher Dawson, *The Tablet*, August 18, 1945, p. 74.

[15]Reinhold Niebuhr, *Does Civilization Need Religion? A Study in the Social Resources and Limitations of Religion in Modern Life* (New York: Macmillan, 1927), p. 166.

[16]Chesterton, *Everlasting Man*, p. 361.

CHAPTER 5: THE DYNAMICS OF THE KINGDOM

[1]Acts 27:24, 34.

[2]Acts 27:44.

[3]Acts 27:31.

[4]Luke 4:4; Deuteronomy 8:3.

[5]Johann Wolfgang von Goethe, "General Confession," in Friedrich Nietzsche, *The Birth of Tragedy*, trans. Douglas Smith (New York: Oxford University Press, 2000), p. 135.

[6]Isaiah 55:8-9.

[7]Blaise Pascal, *Pensées*, trans. A. J. Krailsheimer (New York: Penguin, 1995), p. 66.

[8]See Randall Collins, *A Sociology of Philosophies* (Cambridge, MA: Belknap, 1998).

[9]See Nathan O. Hatch, *The Democratization of American Christianity* (New Haven, CT: Yale University Press, 1989).

[10]1 Corinthians 1.26.

[11]Christopher Dawson, *Beyond Politics* (New York: Sheed & Ward, 1939), p. 127.

[12]Acts 13:2.

[13]Acts 17:6.

[14]T. S. Eliot, *Christianity and Culture* (New York: Harcourt, 1976), p. 170.

[15]Luke 1:51-53.

[16]John Baillie, *What Is Christian Civilization?* (London: Christophers, 1945), p. 60.

[17]Eliot, *Christianity and Culture,* p. 92.

[18]Reinhold Niebuhr, *The Irony of American History* (1952; repr., Chicago: University of Chicago Press, 2008), p. 63.

[19]Eliot, *Christianity and Culture*, p. 196.

[20]Matthew 6:33.

CHAPTER 6: OUR GOLDEN AGE IS AHEAD

[1]Roland Hill, *Lord Acton* (New Haven, CT: Yale University Press, 2011).

[2]Bernard of Clairvaux, *On Consideration,* trans. George Lewis (Oxford: Clarendon, 1908), p. 75 (book 3.1).

[3]Ibid., p. 34 (book 1.10).

[4]1 Kings 12:24.

[5]Christopher Dawson, *The Dividing of Christendom* (San Francisco: Ignatius, 1971), p. 31.

[6]Søren Kierkegaard, *Attack upon "Christendom,"* trans. Walter Lowrie (Princeton, NJ: Princeton University Press, 1968), pp. 32-33.

[7]Cited in Erik von Kuehnelt-Leddihn, *Leftism Revisited: From De Sade to Marx and Hitler to Pol Pot* (Washington, DC: Regnery Gateway, 1990), p. 208.

[8]T. S. Eliot, *Christianity and Culture* (New York: Harcourt, 1976), p. 20, italics original.

[9]Kuehnelt-Leddihn, *Leftism Revisited,* p. 79.

[10]Ibid., p. 336.

[11]Quoted in Christopher Dawson, *The Making of Europe* (Washington, DC: Catholic University of America Press, 1954), p. 41.

[12]Quoted in R. A. Markus, *Saeculum: History and Society in the Theology of St. Augustine* (New York: Cambridge University Press, 1988), p. 164.

[13]William Shakespeare, *Sonnet 94,* line 14.

[14]Robert Hughes, *Rome: A Cultural, Personal, and Visual History* (New York: Knopf, 2011), p. 195.

[15]Kierkegaard, *Attack upon "Christendom,"* p. 167.

[16]Ibid., p. 149.

[17]John Donne, "A Litany," stanza 8, line 1.

[18]Ezekiel 37:3.

[19]Romans 4:17.

CONCLUDING POSTSCRIPT

[1]See Ezekiel 37:3.

[2]Sophocles, *Antigone,* in *The Complete Greek Tragedies: Sophocles,* ed. David Greene and Richmond Lattimore (Chicago, University of Chicago Press, 1959).

[3]Luke 21:28.

[4]Genesis 32:26.

[5]Christopher Dawson, *Progress & Religion* (Washington, DC: Catholic University of America Press, 2001), p. 180.

[6]Emil Brunner, *Christianity and Civilisation*, vol. 1: *Foundations* (London: Nisbet & Co., 1948), p. v.

[7]Christopher Dawson, *Beyond Politics* (New York: Sheed & Ward, 1939), p. 90, italics added.

[8]Psalm 115:1.

[9]Psalm 80:3, 7, 19.

[10]1 Chronicles 12:32.

INTRODUCTION TO AN EVANGELICAL MANIFESTO

[1]The terms *Evangelical* and *Evangelicals* should be spelled with an upper case when referring to people or to the movement, as are the terms Orthodox, Roman Catholic and Protestant, and Jew, Christian and Muslim. The Evangelical Manifesto and supplementary materials are available online at www.anevangelicalmanifesto.com. Copyright ©2008 by the Evangelical Manifesto Steering Committee, used with permission.

[2]C. S. Lewis, "Introduction," in Athanasius, *The Incarnation of the Word of God*, trans. C.S.M.V. (London: Geoffrey Bles, 1944), p. 6.

[3]Athanasius, *Incarnation of the Word*, p. 41.

[4]Quoted in R. A. Markus, *Saeculum: History and Society in the Theology of St. Augustine* (New York: Cambridge University Press, 1988), p. 23

NAME INDEX

Other Titles by Os Guinness

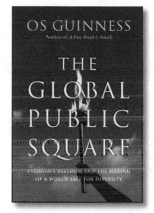

A Free People's Suicide
978-0-8308-3465-5

The Global Public Square
978-0-8308-3767-0

Available at ivpress.com